"Improv symbolizes the kind of mental agility
that every person needs in today's tumultuous times.
Believe me, it's not just a laughing matter."

Allan Weiss, PhD
author of *Million Dollar Consulting*
President, Summit Consulting Group

"The heart of improvisation is to be in your life
with your whole self in it. There's exhilarating energy, waves
of creativity, and enormous insight. What a wondrous gift
for a trainer to give to others and to feel for themselves!"

Peggy Jo Wallis
Wallis, a training, consulting, and mentoring firm

"Once you experience improv, you will embrace it as a tool that
brings teams together, teaches the concept of and appreciation for
building off of what you are given, and, best of all, produces laughter
and fun. Izzy is the personification of the phrase 'lighten-up.'"

Duncan Rowles, facilitator of team and group process
Principal, Pond Associates, LLC

"Improv is the willingness to become completely vulnerable.
In other words, it's being open to all possibilities and then
trusting the outcome. It's the way obstacles are overcome and
it is the most frightening and most rewarding thing I do in
my life. Improv is how people and companies flourish."

Greg Larson, stage actor

"Today's audiences want to be actively involved.
Improvisational exercises involve learners and
are a great way to drive your message home."

Joanne Schlosser, president
Dynamic Presentations
Member of Oxymoron'Z Improvisational Comedy Troupe

pLAYiNg ALONg

37 GROUP LEARNING ACTIVITIES
BORROWED FROM IMPROVISATIONAL THEATER

For Sandra,
With glee at knowing
a fellow traveler on the road to
joyful learning!

Best,
Izzy

WHOLE PERSON ASSOCIATES
Duluth, Minnesota

Whole Person Associates
210 W Michigan
Duluth, MN 55802-1908
800-247-6789

Playing Along:
37 Learning Activities Borrowed from Improvisational Theater

Printed in the United States of America
10 9 8 7 6 5 4 3 2 1

Editorial Director: Susan Gustafson
Art Director: Joy Morgan Dey
Manuscript Editor: Kathy DeArmond-Lundblad

Library of Congress Cataloging-in-Publication Data
Gesell, Izzy.
   Playing along: 37 learning activities borrowed from improvisational theater / Izzy Gesell.
   160 p. 23 cm.
   Includes bibliographical references.
   ISBN 1-57025-141-X
   1. Group relations training—Problems, exercises, etc.
2. Group games. 3. Improvisation (Acting) I. Title.
HM134.G484 1997
302'.14—dc21   96-51245
                                    CIP

DEDICATION

To the memory of my parents who taught me that in order to live you need to be able to improvise.

To Carol who taught me that in order to love and be loved you need to be able to improvise.

To the trainers, consultants, executives, and managers who courageously and enthusiastically welcomed improv techniques into their organizations. You believed in the power of improv before you even experienced it.

To Martin deMaat and the other improv teachers and players I've worked with for showing me the meaning of life by showing me the essence of improv.

Through his entertaining, informative, practical, and customized programs, Izzy helps individuals and organizations harness the physical, mental, emotional, and spiritual power of humor.

Program topics include "Becoming Light-Hearted: Managing stress and change through humor," "Are We on the Same Bus?: Exploring gender differences in communication styles," "Self-Talk: How to stay confident and optimistic in any situation," and "Playing Along: Increasing personal and team effectiveness through improvisational theater skills."

A 50-minute audiotape of "Becoming Lightheated" is available for $12 (include shipping and handling). The tape includes a live performance of Izzy's most requested motivational humor program with additional materials to help everyone reap the benefits of his message.

If you would like information about a keynote address, a half-day workshop, a full day seminar, individualized consultations, presentation and humor coaching, or the audiotape, please contact Izzy at Wide Angel Humor, PO Box 962, Northampton, Massachusetts 01061. Phone: 413-586-2634, Fax: 413-585-0407.

TABLE OF CONTENTS

ACTION!

RESOURCES

ABOUT THE AUTHOR

Izzy Gesell, "America's Humorologist" is Head Honcho of Wide Angle Humor Consultants. Now living in Northampton, Massachusetts, Izzy is originally from Brooklyn, New York, (where a sense of humor is a survival skill). He has a BA in psychology, a MS in education, and a P (that's one third of a PhD) and has been working with humor and play all his adult life as a teacher, stand-up comedian, improv troupe member, corporate trainer, and workshop leader.

In 1988 he founded Wide Angle Humor as a way to help others reap the benefits of an active sense of humor. He has become nationally known as an expert in helping organizations and the people within them thrive, prosper, and become more productive. His clients include Chrysler, Hewlett-Packard, Kaiser Permanente, Lego, and office staff of the United States House of Representatives.

Izzy is the originator of International Moment of Laughter Day, celebrated each April 29, aimed at getting everyone to recognize the physical, emotional, and spiritual power of laughter.

He is the stepfather of two children, the grandfather of one, and the husband of a woman with both a great sense of humor and a ton of patience.

INTRODUCTION

Although the roots of improvisational theater go back to the sixteenth century entertainment form known as commedia dell'arte, the fruits of this art have blossomed into modern improv techniques that are relevant to our lives today. In fact, the problem-solving abilities that make for a successful improv actor are valuable offstage as well.

The modern form of improv was developed to help actors solve problems on stage. I first studied improvisational theater because I believed improv theater players had a magical talent that most others did not. I longed to decipher the mystical code that could allow ordinary people to become fearlessly spontaneous and creatively humorous. First as a student in improv classes and later as a member of a professional improvisation theater group, I discovered the magical skills needed were really not so enchanted after all.

The successful improv player's bag of tricks includes listening to others without prejudgment, accepting what is offered by others, trusting that the group will solve a problem, and letting go of one's own needs to control situations or predetermine outcomes. These capabilities are all developed through improv. Improv players gain confidence to allow their own spontaneity to flow without self-censorship, poise to allow the spontaneity of others to flow without criticism, and belief in their ability to solve problems. This is why sales people, trainers, factory workers, managers, nurses, teachers, and homemakers can all benefit from experiencing improv.

In improv, the exercises are often called structures or games. As the names indicate, the exercises have rules, or parameters, which guide the players. It is possible, indeed often desirable, for players to bend the rules. Yet as long as all players are following the same rules (or all bending them in the same direction), the game moves forward and therefore is successful.

Many people mistakenly believe that to be successful at improv they must think quickly. The most common desire of those who take my Improvisational Theater Skills workshops is to learn to think quickly on their feet. In truth, improv does help quick-wittedness, but its power lies in physical rather than verbal spontaneity. Success comes from paying attention to the body, not the head. Obstacles to success consist mainly of self-doubt and self-consciousness. Because we fear looking foolish, we screen our impulses. Keith Johnstone, author of *IMPRO*, believes 95 percent of us think our spontaneous responses—those first thoughts out of our heads and mouths—are "crazier" than what others would come up with. We censor ourselves in order to appear normal. In improv, honest, impulsive responses are more effective than calculated, deliberate ones.

Invite players to allow their bodies to guide them in every situation. Solutions lie in actions, not words. Encourage them to cry rather than to say they are sad; to drink glass after glass of water rather than pronounce "I'm thirsty." Players do not need to think. They need to be.

Within the games, the participants, referred to as players, create the environment which contains their reality. In a real sense, the power of improv lies in being in the moment at all times. The next action is always in sight and close at hand. Getting to that next step, however, may be difficult because of the blocking influence of thought and our low tolerance for looking silly. The solution lies within the structure of the game being played. The structure provides a path around and through the obstacles.

The focal point of each game is what Viola Spolin, author of *Improvisation for the Theater*, defines as the point of concentration. A key concept in improv, the point of concentration requires close attention to the problem rather than to the individuals who are addressing the problem. In volleyball, for example, the ball is the point of concentration. Each individual player, as a member of a team, must focus on the ball and act in collaboration with teammates. By attending to the point of concentration, players avoid self-consciousness. Whenever an improv participant flounders, remind them of the point of concentration.

Many people believe that they and most others don't know how to improvise. To that I say, "balderdash" or some equivalent phrase. Unless someone writes a script for our lives and leaves it on the night stand, we improvise each and every day.

Successful improvisers don't deliberately try to be funny. Actually, working at being funny often leads to failure—in life as well as in improv. Amusement is most often derived from the humor found in real-life. Laughter follows when we discover the incongruity between our expectations and actual events. As the authors of *Truth in Comedy* point out, "honest discovery, observation, and reaction is better than contrived invention." I believe this is also true in our personal and organizational lives.

In improv, players learn that reality, or truth, has texture, space, depth, and substance. Players must create physical reality through individual action and emotion while at the same time, they develop a shared vision with other players. The magic in this creation of reality is evident when people begin to understand how "true" reality is created and how beliefs, doubts, self-talk, and preconceptions determine what happens to us. The goal for participants in these exercises is to be real, not to be acting.

The games or structures in this book will be organic and alive. Each time you offer a structure, you will experience a different reality. Each reality will be born of the situations presented and the players involved. You and the players will discover new insights as you discuss the connections between the reality they experienced in the structure and their real lives. I encourage you to note these as they come up and use them in your ever-growing understanding of how improv exercises help us live more effective, confident, and "in-the-moment" lives. I hope you will see why I consider improv to be "a ropes course for the mind."

Each of the games can be played again and again. Groups will gain confidence and increased skills as exercises are repeated. You, too, will find the cumulative effect of improv will transform the way you experience yourself and view the world.

A final reminder. The concept of fun is not to be underestimated. Improv is a lot of fun. If you are having fun, then the participants will have fun.

As we begin, I offer the following excerpt from improvisation theater pioneer Viola Spolin who explains how improv can be a powerful tool for helping people take control of their lives at the same time they are having a tremendous amount of fun.

> "It stands to reason that if we direct all of our efforts towards reaching a goal, we stand in danger of losing everything on which we have based our daily activities. For when a goal

is superimposed on an activity instead of evolving out of it, we often feel cheated when we reach it."

"When the goal appears easily and naturally and comes from growth rather than forcing, the end-result will be no different than the process that achieved the result. If we are trained only for success, then to gain it we must necessarily use everything for this end; cheat, lie, betray, give up all social life to achieve success. How much more certain would knowledge be if it came from and out of the excitement of learning itself. How many human values will be lost and how much will our art forms be deprived if we seek only success?"

I would love to hear about your experiences using these techniques. You will have insights, happenings, outcomes, questions, and applications that can help others use and understand improv. I would be delighted to answer your questions.

In addition, if you'd like to be part of the growing network of people who love the fun and transformational properties of improv, send your name, mailing address, and/or e-mail address to me, and I will do my best to keep you posted. I don't know exactly what is going to happen, but I know it will be wonderful. Please address all correspondence to:

Izzy Gesell
Wide Angle Humor
PO Box 962
Northampton, MA 01061

BASIC IMPROV

If you are not familiar with improvisational theater, the following guidelines may be helpful. But don't be concerned about getting it all perfect. Just jump right in and give it a try.

GUIDELINES FOR INSTRUCTORS

Because much of improv is physical, stretching and other preparation for physical activity will be helpful. Include vocal warm-ups to stretch vocal cords and encourage enthusiasm and exuberance. These activities also reduce self-consciousness.

To reinforce the understanding that the group is involved in theater, position yourself as the emcee or master of ceremonies as much as possible and refer to the participants in the session as players and audience members.

Don't push people to perform but encourage them. Ask players to volunteer and inform them that they will not be pressured to participate. Large group activities make it easier for reluctant players to get involved.

HINTS FOR PLAYERS

The only rule that must be followed is the rule of agreement, which states "I agree to accept any reality offered within a structure and will commit to that reality without a moment's hesitation."

Accept any offer that is given to you as player or emcee. It is improv etiquette to use the first suggestion you hear.

Make unusual choices. If you have two options, choose the unfamiliar one even if it seems uncomfortable. Unusual choices make for great improv.

Making large actions and overt gestures is called playing "big." Make "big" choices when you move or take action.

Conflict and action make scenes interesting.

If you feel stuck or frightened, don't think about what to do next. Instead, become silent, take a couple of deep breaths, and focus on your body position. Allow your body position to guide your next action.

The following ideas will be helpful if players seem to be floundering. Make active statements rather than asking open-ended questions. For example, if you pick something off the floor say, "What a beautiful diamond" instead of asking your partner, "What do you think this is?" The statement helps your partner and allows the action to move forward.

Don't think about what you will do.

Don't anticipate what others are going to do.

Don't worry about making mistakes because if something doesn't work, we just move on to something else.

THE FORMAT OF THE GAMES

Description: The title of each game is followed by a brief description, which is repeated in the section divider pages.

Goals: A common goal in every game is to have fun. Other goals are potential benefits for players. They are by no means the only benefits to be had. You will discover more in the discussions.

Group size: A group size of two means two at a time can play. Most games can be played more than once in a session with different people.

Time: The time indicated is the minimum needed to introduce the game, play it once, and engage in discussion. It will take less time to repeat the game with new players.

Process: Complete guidelines are given for presenting the games to the players. Adapt them as needed for your groups.

Discussion questions: The questions will spark insight and understanding for you and the players and will help you extend those insights to daily life. Many questions can be used with most of the games. Universal questions include: What were the obstacles to success? What behaviors overcame the obstacles? How did you feel at the beginning? At the end?

Variations: Simple variations allow you to present the same basic game with a different twist.

GLOSSARY

Audience: Those who are observing a scene. The audience in improv is very important. Audience members have as much fun as participants on stage. In many of the games, audience members quickly become players and players become audience members. Not all games differentiate between audience and players.

Emcee: The person who introduces the game, gives the instructions, moderates the action, and gets the suggestions from the audience. It may be the facilitator or any group member.

Game: Another word for an improv structure, activity, or exercise. Use of this word reinforces the importance of having fun while experiencing improv. It is also a reminder that improv activities have rules. In any game, the goal for each player is to play by the same rules as every other player. The rules may shift, yet as long as all players agree to them, the game continues.

Gibberish: Nonsense sounds used in a conversational manner to help players communicate nonverbally.

Natural end point: A convenient place to end a scene or interaction between players. It may be when the allotted time runs out; it may be when the scene is chaotic and you can't imagine it getting back on track; or it may be any place in the action where a filmmaker would use a blackout or fade. In improv, players very often have the right and the obligation to end a scene themselves.

Offer: A question or statement that gives a player an opportunity to respond. A cardinal rule of improv is to accept any offer. If two players are in a scene that takes place on the Titanic and a third enters and says, "What's that camel doing out there?" the players should accept the offer and may say, "I didn't realize we'd drifted so far south. Let's get on it and ride to safety." This response incorporates the offer into the scene and allows the action to continue. The players may instead block the offer which means denying the offer by rejecting or ignoring what was given. "That can't be a camel. We're near the North Pole," is a blocking answer and stops the action while throwing the players out of alignment with each other.

Player: A participant in an activity.

Scene: The setting in which the players play the game. A scene sets parameters so all know who the players are supposed to be and where the action is taking place.

Setting up a scene: Getting information from the audience or from players that gives context to what will follow. Questions that help set up a scene are, "Who are these people? What is their relationship to each other? Where are they? In addition, you may ask for the first or last line of the scene.

Stage: The area where the players are and the audience is not. For our purposes, the stage need not be raised or marked off. Not all games use a stage area.

Structure: Another word for a game, exercise, or activity. The word refers to the rules governing each improv event. It also belies the belief that improv is always without boundaries.

LIGHTS!

Improv illuminates understandings that seem paradoxical. For example, improv works on the premise that without structure there is no freedom and that if you practice spontaneity, you become a spontaneous person.

WHO'S IN CHARGE HERE?

 *A player, who stands in the center of a circle formed by the other players, must discover which of the other players is leading the group activities.*

GOALS

To warm up the group.

To encourage players to look at each other, which contributes to them loosening up and feeling comfortable with each other.

To work as an ensemble.

GROUP SIZE

10–25 players.

TIME

5–10 minutes.

PROCESS

▦ Arrange the players in a circle, either standing or sitting.

▦ Choose a volunteer as Player 1 and have that person stand in the center of the circle.

■ Give the following instructions:

▲ Player 1, when I say so, close your eyes.

▲ While your eyes are closed, I will select a leader, Player 2, from the players in the circle by pointing to that person. Player 2 will acknowledge acceptance by nodding.

▲ Player 2, as leader, your job is to guide the other players through a series of motions.

▲ You will do this without speaking, by demonstrating what you'd like the rest of the group to do. For example, if you want them to clap their hands, start clapping your hands. If you want them to rub their noses, do so yourself.

▲ The objective is to keep changing the actions while preventing Player 1 from determining who is in charge.

▲ Player 2, you may change actions at any time, even while Player 1 is looking at you.

▲ Group, continue the action until you see the leader, or any other player, change the motion. Then, immediately and smoothly, pick up on the new movement.

▲ You do not have to look at the leader. You can look at any other player. If you see any player change motion, you will know that the leader has initiated that change.

▲ The game will continue until Player 1 either discovers who the leader is or makes wrong guesses. If Player 1 picks the correct person, Player 2 comes into the center for the next round. If the choices are incorrect, two different players will be chosen for the next round.

■ Begin the game and continue for as many rounds as you like.

■ Conclude the activity with the following questions:

▲ As the player in the center, what tactics did you use to distinguish the leader from the followers?

▲ Did you change strategies during the game? If so, what prompted the changes?

▲ How did you feel during the game?

▲ Leader, as the person in charge, what tactics did you employ to keep Player 2 from finding you?

▲ As followers, what tactics did you use to follow the motion while keeping Player 1 from discovering the leader?

▲ How did it feel to be part of this group working together on an enjoyable task?

SLAP, CLAP, SNAP

 *The entire group develops a rhythmic activity by slapping their thighs, clapping their hands, and snapping their fingers. Once the rhythm is sustained, a word association game is added.*

GOALS

To stay in the moment.
To enhance concentration.
To improve listening skills.

GROUP SIZE

5–15 players. An unlimited number of players can engage in the third variation.

TIME

5–20 minutes.

PROCESS

▓ Arrange the players, standing and in a circle.

▓ Introduce the game as one in which all players work together to establish a rhythm using their hands and thighs.

■ Stand in the center of the circle and give the following instructions while demonstrating:

▲ Begin a rhythm by slapping the front of your thighs twice with both your hands, then clapping twice, then snapping the fingers on both your hands in unison twice.

▲ Remember, its hands on thighs for two counts, clap hands for two counts, snap fingers for two counts. Everybody follow along at the same beat: slap-slap, clap-clap, snap-snap.

■ When the group can sustain the beat, give the following additional instructions:

▲ I am going to point to one of you. When I do, it will become your turn to say a word on the second snap of the fingers. It can be any word. Don't think about it, just say a word on the second snap. If it was my turn, I might say "ball." It would sound like this: Slap-slap, clap-clap, snap-snap with the word ball coinciding with the second snap.

▲ Once Player 1 states the word, the person to the left of Player 1, has until the second snap of the next series to come up with a word that begins with the last letter of Player 1's word. Using our example, Player 2 may say love." It would sound like this: Slap-slap, clap-clap, snap-snap with the word love coinciding with the second snap.

▲ We will go around the circle in this manner. Words cannot be repeated and each word must be said on the second snap.

■ Continue until everyone in the circle has had a turn. If the game is too easy, quicken the cadence.

■ Conclude the game with a discussion of the following questions:

▲ Is it hard to concentrate on more than one thing at a time?

▲ What conditions are necessary to foster a team spirit?

▲ In improv, every choice you make affects at least one other person. Discuss how this is relevant to a situation in your life.

VARIATIONS

▦ Quicken the rhythm by slapping, clapping, and snapping once instead of twice. The cadence then is slap-clap-snap instead of slap-slap, clap-clap, snap-snap. In this version, the word is stated on the snap.

▦ A competitive version can be played by eliminating any player who repeats a word, uses a word that doesn't begin with the last letter of the previous word, or doesn't get the word out on the right beat.

▦ Use the rhythmic portion by itself, eliminating the word association. This variation is useful as a warm-up or icebreaker when time is short or the risk-taking level of the group is low.

YES!!!

 In this highly energetic game, players, in unison, mime a succession of physical activities. Each activity is prefaced by a unified chorus of "yes!"

GOALS
To accept others' ideas and offers unconditionally.
To follow through on agreements.
To lose feelings of self-consciousness.
To build enthusiasm within a group.

GROUP SIZE
Unlimited.

TIME
5 minutes.

> *Make sure room space is adequate for players to move around comfortably without bumping into each other. With limited room space, form a circle and have players mime activities in place or within the circle.*

PROCESS

▦ Introduce the goals of the exercise and provide the following instructions to players:

▲ We are going to play a game called **Yes!!!**.

If space is limited, eliminate the following instruction, form a circle, and begin the game with the suggestion in the second instruction.

▲ To begin the game, stroll around the room for 45 seconds. Wander aimlessly, imagining that it's a beautiful day, you have time to kill, and you have no particular place you need to hurry to. Stroll in any direction; double back or zigzag; any pattern you choose is okay.

▲ After you stroll about the room for a few minutes, I will suggest a physical activity in a loud, enthusiastic voice. For example, I may say "Let's go sky diving!"

▲ When I suggest the activity, I would like everyone in the room to immediately, enthusiastically, and loudly shout "yes!"

▲ At that time, begin to pantomime the suggested activity, in this case sky diving. I want to see everyone in the room sky diving!

▲ We will continue the activity while others in the group take turns offering other activities by calling them out. For example, someone may call out "Let's have a cup of tea!"

▲ At that time, we will all stop sky diving and immediately, enthusiastically, and loudly shout "yes!" Everyone immediately begins drinking tea and continues this activity until another suggestion is made. Any group member can make a suggestion at any time.

▲ During this activity, stay enthusiastic and participate in each suggestion wholeheartedly in any way you desire. Don't worry about how others are doing it.

■ After the instructions are given to the group, begin the game. Continue through four or five group members' suggestions or as long as time allows.

■ When the game is finished, reconvene the entire group and lead players in a discussion using some of the following questions:

▲ Did you feel self-conscious at all? If so, why?

▲ Did you ever lose the feeling of being self-conscious? If so, when and how?

■ Ask participants to share any insights they gained during this activity.

BALL TOSS

In this energetic exercise, players create reality by using the physical signals of throwing and catching an imaginary ball.

GOALS

To create a shared reality through physical action.

To warm up a group.

GROUP SIZE

Unlimited.

TIME

5 minutes.

PROCESS

■ Introduce the goals of the exercise to the group. Arrange the players in a circle and introduce the activity using the following statement:

▲ In this exercise, we will be throwing an imaginary ball to one another for several minutes. As we do so, you will learn firsthand that body movements and sounds as well as shared assumptions about the nature of the imaginary ball will make it seem real.

▪ Select a participant to be Player 1 and give the following instructions to the entire group:

▲ To begin this game, Player 1 will throw the ball to any other player in the circle. Since we don't really have a ball, Player 1 must decide what kind of ball it is. The weight, size, shape, and purpose of the ball will help you decide how to throw it to the second player.

▲ Player 1, before you throw the ball call out the name of the person you are throwing to and the kind of ball you are throwing. For example, make eye contact and say before you throw: "Player 2, a football" or "Player 2, a ping-pong ball."

In the event that the players don't know each other's names, be sure to tell them to make eye contact with the intended receiver before they throw the ball.

▲ Player 2, catch the ball as it comes to you.

▲ Player 2 now prepares to throw the ball to a third player. Be sure you change the nature of the ball before you throw it to Player 3. If you received a tennis ball, roll a bowling ball or throw a beach ball across to the next player.

▲ Players, as you are throwing or receiving the imaginary ball, bring your entire body into the action. When you are the thrower, throw it with your entire body. When you are the receiver, catch it with more than just your hands.

▲ Use the weight, function, and size of the ball to guide your motions and reactions. Keep your attention focused on the ball as it travels and reaches another person.

- Continue the game for 5 minutes or until the group has loosened up.

- Reconvene the group and lead a closing discussion using the following questions:

  - What makes the ball seem real to you?

  - Is it possible for your body to respond to a make-believe ball in the same way as it does to a real one?

  - How is this possible? Or is it not possible?

VARIATIONS

- **Sound toss:** Instruct players to form a circle. Ask the first player to throw a sound across the circle to a second player. The second player receives the sound by repeating it and giving a whole body response, then throws a different sound to a third player who catches it, changes it, and throws it to a fourth. Continue the game until everyone has had a turn.

- **Passing face:** Ask players to form a circle. The first player begins by making a face that signifies an emotion, then passes that emotion to the next person in the circle. That person copies the facial expression, then turns and passes it to the next player, transforming the face into something different. The third player accepts the facial gesture and changes it again. Continue this process around the circle.

ECHO

 Players experience team interdependence as they pass a sound from one player to another until it fades away.

GOALS
To practice vocal agility.
To experience team interdependence.

GROUP SIZE
Two teams of 5–15 players each.

TIME
2–3 minutes.

PROCESS

▪ Introduce the goals of the exercise and form two groups. Have participants count off by twos or choose another method to form the groups.

▪ Ask the two teams to line up single file as if to start a tug-of-war. Give the following instructions for the activity:

▲ The purpose of this activity is to quickly pass a sound from person to person down the team line so that it fades away as it reaches the last player in the line. It should sound like an echo bouncing between cliffs as it fades away.

▲ To get started, I would like the player at the front of Team 1 to loudly call out a word or phrase of your choice.

▲ Beginning with the player at the front of Team 2, the word or phrase is repeated in turn by each player on Team 2 without pause.

▲ Remember, the object of this activity is to gradually diminish the volume so the word or phrase finally fades away at the end of the team line.

▲ When Team 2 completes the echo, the player at the front of Team 2 will then call out a word or phrase for Team 1 to echo.

▲ The player at the front of Team 1 will repeat the word or phrase loudly and pass it along to the next player. It is repeated in turn by each player on Team 1 until it fades away as it reaches the last player in the line.

■ Continue the game, alternating between the two teams for a few rounds or as time allows. In the ensuing rounds, ask players 2, 3 . . . to offer the word or phrase.

■ Use some of the following questions to elicit discussion.

▲ Did you find that you could respond without thinking?

▲ In what other situations might a suspension of thought be useful?

▲ What was going through your mind while waiting for the sound to come to you?

FOLD THE BLANKET

 Group members engage in a cooperative activity around an object which is not really there.

GOALS
To create a shared reality through team agreement.
To share a common vision.
To create something out of nothing.

GROUP SIZE
Unlimited.

TIME
10 minutes.

> *Make sure that each team will have their own space with enough room to fold an imaginary blanket.*

PROCESS
◼ Introduce the goals of the exercise, then form teams of three or four participants.

◼ Instruct each team to find an open space and to move to that area. Read aloud the following sentences, pausing long enough for participants to respond to each statement.

You are on a beach with some friends.
A large blanket is spread on the sand.
Sit down on your blanket and enjoy the sun, sand, and surf.
Oh, oh! A rain storm is rapidly approaching.
As a team, fold your blanket and get ready to leave the beach.

As participants are getting ready to fold their blanket, remind them of the following points:

- The goal of this activity is to simply get the blanket folded. This isn't a competition nor a race.

- Focus your attention on your own blanket and the actions of your teammates.

- You will have 1–2 minutes for this process.

While the teams are folding their blanket, notice any differences among the teams.

Some groups will be in sync and organized. They will work together, and it will be evident when they've finished folding the blanket.

Some groups will be working at odds with each other. It will look as if there were more than one blanket in the group.

If no group has completed the task within 2 minutes, ask participants to try for a little while longer. Tell them they can start from the beginning by dropping the blanket onto the sand and picking it up again. Most likely, at least one group will have completed the task within 2 minutes.

Reconvene the entire group and use the following questions to prompt a discussion:

▲ Those who folded the blanket, how did you know you were done since there isn't a real blanket anywhere to be seen?

▲ What actions did you take, individually and jointly, that helped you succeed?

▲ Those who didn't finish folding the blanket, what prevented you from completing the task?

▲ What techniques did you try, individually and jointly, to overcome the obstacles?

▲ All players, what feelings and emotions came up during the game?

▪ Lead a discussion by making the following points and asking participants to share any additional comments or insights they gained during this activity:

▲ The reality of folding a blanket is not created by actually having a blanket but rather through a common view and complementary actions by the group.

▲ The essence of reality is created through action and agreement of all the team players. In essence, reality is a shared vision among people.

▪ Ask the group to brainstorm ways this approach can help us deal with change in our everyday life. Can we learn to participate in another person's reality even if we don't understand it?

VARIATION

▪ **Bathe the puppy:** This exercise has the same objective as **Fold the blanket**: creating shared, cooperative reality. It is also effective as a follow-up to **Fold the blanket** as players can put newly learned concepts into practice.

TICKY, TICKY, TOCK

 *The group forms a circle. When pointed to by the leader, a trio of players join to create a designated animal or person within a very short period of time.*

GOALS
To energize a group.
To enhance working together.
To experience feeling confident and nonjudgmental.

GROUP SIZE
Unlimited.

TIME
10–20 minutes.

PROCESS
▨ Arrange the group in a circle.

▨ Stand in the center of the circle and give the group the following instructions:

- I am going to point to a player and say one of the following words: elephant, fighter pilot, or eagle. Working with the players on your immediate left and immediate right, you will create the character I mentioned.

- If I ask for an elephant, Player 1 display the trunk of an elephant by holding one arm straight out in front of you and grasping the elbow of that arm with your other hand. Wave your outstretched arm. If I ask for a fighter pilot, create the flight goggles by putting the thumb and forefinger of each hand together forming a circle and placing the goggles against your eyes. If I ask for an eagle, create its beak by hooking both forefingers and holding them against your nose.

- Players 2 and 3, on either side of Player 1, must complete the picture. As elephant ears, Player 2, to the left of Player 1, raise your left hand, bend your left elbow, and lean toward Player 1 so your hand becomes the elephant's ear. Player 3, to the right of Player 1, do the same with your right hand.

- As fighter plane wings, Players 2 and 3 should hold their outside arms stiff and out to the side.

- As eagle wings, Players 2 and 3 should gracefully wave their outside arms.

- You have a very short time to do this: you must complete the tableau before I finish saying "ticky, ticky, tock." If a player performs an incorrect movement or the team doesn't finish in the allotted time, Player 1 comes to the center of the circle, points to the next Player 1, and chooses the next scene.

- Let's practice a bit.

From the middle of the circle, go up to any player, point, and say "elephant." As soon as possible after you say elephant, say "ticky ticky, tock." If the players have not assumed a reasonable facsimile of the elephant by the time you say "tock," trade places with the middle player. That player must now go to any other player, point, and say either elephant, fighter pilot, or eagle.

■ Continue the game for about 5 minutes or until time runs out. Remind the player in the center to say "ticky, ticky, tock." Otherwise, the three players do not have to hurry to get into position. Remember, they should be racing against time.

■ This game generates much enthusiasm, laughter, and silliness. Players may try very hard to "win," that is, not to be put into the center. Suggest to those players that this is a game where it is as much fun to lose as it is to win.

■ Conclude the activity with the following questions:

▲ Was it hard to get into the flow of this game?

▲ Did you think a lot about whether you were as good at this game as other players?

▲ When you are playing, did you feel very much in the moment: confident, open, unattached to the outcome, and full of energy? Does that have implications for your daily life?

VARIATIONS

■ Place two or more players in the center roaming within the circle. This creates a joyful, chaotic sense in the game.

■ Make up your own creatures and three-person tableaus. Consider a dog, scuba diver, duck, or rabbit.

MIRROR, MIRROR

 *Players experience synchronistic movement as they pair up with a partner and imitate each others actions like a reflection in a mirror.*

GOALS

To listen with your body and to respond synchronistically. To loosen up physically.

GROUP SIZE

Unlimited.

TIME

10–15 minutes.

PROCESS

▦ Introduce the goals of the exercise and ask players to select a partner. If there is an odd number of participants in the group, you can pair up with the extra person so everyone has a partner.

▦ When everyone has a partner, give the following instructions:

▲ In each pair, decide who will begin. That person will be

Player 1, the initiator of the movement. Your partner, Player 2, will act as a mirror, reflecting all your movements, including your facial expressions.

▲ Player 1, when I say so, begin a series of movements with your body. You may act out some behavior, such as brushing your teeth, or you may make random movements with your hands, face, feet, or other body parts. You may use all of your body. You don't have to remain standing; you don't have to remain in one place.

▲ Player 2, you will act as a mirror, precisely reflecting Player 1's actions. Player 1, if you raise your right hand then Player 2, raise your left hand in response. Guard against assumptions which prevent mirroring. If Player 1 puts on a shoe, don't assume the next move will be to tie it because of your familiarity with the action.

▲ After 1 minute of mirroring, I will call "change." Players will reverse roles with Player 2 becoming the initiator and Player 1 the mirror.

▲ After 1 minute, I will again call "change" and players will switch roles again. Changes should be made without stoppage of flow in movement. Mirror your partner's actions exactly.

▲ Players will switch roles each time I call "change." Now let's begin the process.

▨ After several switches, add the following instructions:

▲ I now want each player to become both leader and reflector at the same time.

▲ Become so in tune with your partner that an outside observer would be hard-pressed to know who was leading at any time.

■ After the final mirror sequence, lead a closing discussion using the following questions:

▲ Is there a difference between being the initiator and the mirror? If so, what was it?

▲ Which role was easier for you? Why?

▲ What made this activity difficult for you?

▲ What role did your thinking play in helping or hindering you during this exercise?

VARIATION

■ **Who's the mirror?:** One pair of players at a time participates. The rest of the group becomes the audience. The audience must guess which player is the mirror and which is the initiator. Before the game begins, the two players should decide between themselves which is which. One player initiates all the movements while the other player reflects them. The game is played exactly as in **Mirror, mirror** except no one calls "change." When the players are moving, call out the name of one of the players and ask the audience members to raise their hands if they believe that player is the mirror. Next, call out the name of the other player and let the audience vote for that player with a show of hands. Both players continue mirroring during the voting process, which ends when the vote is unanimous in favor of one player.

MONSTER TALK

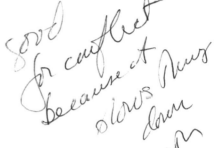

 Two players attempt to say the same words at the same time by slowing their speech down while exaggerating their facial actions.

GOALS

To connect and communicate with another person.
To listen intently.
To work and think together.

GROUP SIZE

Unlimited. 2 players at a time.

TIME

5–10 minutes.

PROCESS

▦ Bring a volunteer player to the stage.

▦ Introduce the activity as one in which you and Player 1 will have a conversation, speaking the same words at the same time. If the group is familiar with the **Mirror, mirror** game, identify this as similar except that words rather than movements will be mirrored.

- Inform the group that you and Player 1 will demonstrate the technique before the others get to experience it themselves.

- Face Player 1 and give the following instructions:

  - I am now starting to speak. You must mirror my speech exactly word for word. I will continue to slooooowwwwww mmmmyyyyy speeeeeechhhhhhh dooooownnnnn untillll youuuuuuu cannnnnn folllll low ev ver eeeee sylllll abbble. Unnnn derrr stannnnd?

  - I want you to pay such close attention to me and what I am saying that the audience will hear both of us saying the same thing at the same time. This activity is called Monster Talk because, as I slow my speech down, I will exaggerate my facial features. You will be able to use my lips, nose, eyes, and mouth to help you synchronize our speech.

  - Keep your focus and concentration intently on my face. Do not anticipate what I will say.

  - Since we are having a conversation, you will want to speak also. You might want to reply to a question, respond to a statement, or make a point. When you do, I will mirror you as you did me. When the lead switches, the conversation should continue uninterrupted. Our goal is to have the audience hear us in stereo.

- Demonstrate the technique with Player 1 until a synchronized conversation between the two of you is achieved.

- Instruct the rest of the group to pair up and begin a conversation using the Monster Talk techniques.

■ Conclude the activity after 2–3 minutes and conclude with the following questions:

▲ How did Monster Talk affect communication?

▲ Did you find yourself anticipating what would be said?

▲ When we listen intently without preconceptions, we avoid misinterpretations. In what ways could intent listening be helpful to you?

VARIATION

■ To help create effective partnerships in a team or department, pair each player with several partners. After several rounds of Monster Talk, ask players to evaluate their comfort and effectiveness with each partner.

GIVE AND TAKE

 *Players practice using nonverbal communication skills, trusting others by alternately moving and then stopping, guided by another player's actions.*

GOALS

To practice relaxation, concentration, and nonverbal communication. To practice trusting, working with others, being spontaneous, and respecting others' pace.

GROUP SIZE

3–6 players at a time.

TIME

10–25 minutes.

PROCESS

▓ Introduce the goals of the exercise to the entire group. Select one volunteer to be Player 1. Provide the following instructions:

   ▲ During this exercise, we are going to play a game that involves moving and stopping. During this game, only one person can be in motion or speaking at any one time.

- Since only one player can be moving at any time, when I'm moving, Player 1 must stand stationary and motionless.

- When I stop moving, that is a signal for Player 1 to start.

- Player 1, if you decide to move before I have stopped, you may do so, but then I must stop.

- Let's demonstrate. Player 1, begin to move while I am already moving. When I see Player 1 begin to move, I'll freeze until Player 1 stops.

Demonstrate the game with Player 1 for 1 minute, highlighting the two origins of movement—a player's own desire to start and another player's desire to stop.

To make the game more complex, select two more volunteers to be Players 2 and 3. Ask them to join Player 1 and add the following instructions:

- We've added two more players to the game but the basic rule remains the same. One person, but only one person, must be in motion at all times.

- To make the activity more interesting, we are going to also add speech to the game by allowing one player at a time to speak. Any one player may move and speak at the same time.

- Speech will work the same as movement. When Player 1 is speaking, Players 2 and 3 must be frozen.

- If Player 2 or 3 begins to move or speak, the other players must freeze.

- We will play the game with a total of three to six players.

Before demonstrating the first round of the game, ask the audience for a situation in which three people might find themselves.

Examples include: a family reunion, an airport terminal, or a personnel office.

■ After a situation has been selected by the group, add more players to complete the team, up to a maximum of six players at a time.

■ Before beginning the first round of the game, provide the following instructions to the team players:

▲ The goal of the game is to establish a flow between players so it appears as if an invisible energy source travels between them.

▲ While playing this game, it is important to move your entire bodies.

▲ We will continue the game until you either show an understanding of the give-and-take nature of the process or are totally out of sync with each other.

▲ Remember to pay attention to each other's state of motion or immobility.

■ After 3–5 minutes, bring up new teams of three to six players and use suggestions from the audience to create new scenarios. Continue to lead additional teams through the activity as long as time permits.

■ Reconvene the entire group and lead a closing discussion using the following questions:

▲ What combination of senses did the players need in order to align with each other?

▲ As a player, what feelings did you experience when someone else made you give up your sound or motion? Was it difficult or easy for you?

- How did you feel when you made the decision to take the motion away from someone else? Was it difficult or easy for you?

- What benefits would this technique bring to you in the workplace, your family, and in your relationships?

- How does this game apply to real-world behavior?

HAND DANCE

 Participants, in pairs and without touching each other, use their arms and hands to jointly create movement.

GOALS
To feel energy flow from person to person.
To reveal the capacity of nonverbal communication.
To experience nonthreatening physical intimacy.

GROUP SIZE
Entire group in pairs.

TIME
10–25 minutes.

PROCESS
▪ Pair off participants and have them stand silently facing each other.

▪ Give the following instructions:

▲ Stand far enough apart so you can barely touch each other with outstretched arms.

▲ Close your eyes and let your head fall forward so your chin rests on your chest.

▲ Let your arms and hands hang loosely and relaxed at your side.

▲ Leaving your chin on your chest, open your eyes. You should be looking down into the space between you and the other player.

▲ Imagine you are a marionette and your right hand has a string attached to it. Let that string lift your hand so that it floats waist-high in the space between you and your partner. Feel the weight of your hand. Feel the buoyancy.

▲ Now imagine your right hand is a kite. Let your kite fly within your space. Allow it to glide in association with your partner's kite.

Allow the kites to fly for a few seconds, then give the following instructions.

▲ Imagine your right hand is a bird. Feel its freedom and desire to soar. Allow the two birds to fly in the same shared space, but without touching each other.

▲ Now, allow the left hand to join the dance without touching any other hand.

▲ Keeping all four hands in your field of vision, let each one become a organism with a life of its own as it dances with its three partners.

▲ Feel the energy flowing through the space from hand to hand.

- Neither player is the leader. Each move is in response to the motion and energy flow from the other hands.

- Allow the dance to continue in silence for 3–4 minutes. Encourage players to move their hands in relation to the movement of the other hands instead of merely copying or mirroring them. Invite them to allow the leadership to flow between them instead of permitting one player to dominate. Prompt them to focus on their hands and not allow other parts of the body to become involved in the action.

- After 3 or 4 minutes, give the following further instructions:

    - Allow your hands to move back towards your chest now. Point your fingers upward with your palms facing but not touching those of your partner. Keep your eyes focused on your hands.

    - Imagine you and your partner are pressing your hands against the opposite sides of a wall. Let that wall get thinner and thinner until your fingertips touch those of your partner. Now, press your palms together as well. Feel the energy in your hands. Stay focused on your hands.

    - Look up and make eye contact with your partner. Hold that for a few seconds. Now silently, and with only your hands and eyes, thank your partner for the dance.

    - Drop your hands and step back when it feels right.

- Allow 30 seconds to 1 minute at the end of the exercise for players to remain within themselves or with their partners. Some will be silent, some will hug each other, some will walk away.

- Conclude the experience by having players sit and explore the following questions:

▲ Did you make any discoveries during the experience?

▲ Was this experience easy or hard for you? Explain.

▲ What was communicated between you and your partner? How do you know what this was?

VARIATIONS

▨ Pair people off with someone they know least in the group or with someone they have difficulty working with or with someone they will need to work with in the future.

▨ Combine pairs into groups of four.

▨ Combine pairs into larger groups. Have people move their hands above their heads with more than four people in a group.

THE SPOTLIGHT

 In this energizing exercise, group members, inspired by a general theme, create a musical pattern of ideas using lines from real songs.

GOALS

To energize the group.

To participate in a game where the whole (the game) is more important than any of the parts (the individual players).

To experience offering complete support.

GROUP SIZE

Unlimited.

TIME

10–20 minutes.

PROCESS

▧   Arrange a group of between six and fifteen players in a semi-circle around an imaginary spotlight and ask them to face the audience. Ask the team for a volunteer to go first, Player 1.

■ Before beginning the activity, ask the audience for a general theme or subject, such as love, work, vacation, or transportation, to use in this game. Give the players the following instructions:

▲ When I say begin, I would like Player 1 to step firmly into the spotlight and begin singing a song sparked by the audience-suggested theme. For example, if the theme is transportation, you might start with "I'm leaving on a jet plane, don't know when I'll be back again." Singing must be loud and confident.

▲ Before Player 1 finishes the second line of the song, Player 2, who can be any player, will literally push Player 1 out of the spotlight and confidently and loudly begin singing a different song, one that was inspired by the one just heard. In this example, it may be related to planes ("Coming in on a wing and a prayer"), transportation of another sort ("Baby, you can drive my car") or being alone ("Since my baby left me").

▲ A third player then immediately interrupts with a different song that's similar in theme to the previous one and is also connected to the overall theme in some manner.

▲ We will continue this pattern at a rapid pace, with players bumping each other out of the spotlight. The spotlight should not be on the singer for more than two lines.

▲ It is all right for song lines to be repeated as that will allow the theme pattern to easily continue.

▲ Don't wait until you have a song in mind before entering the spotlight. Take the risk and jump in. It is an excellent way to support your teammates, it saves a player who is stuck too long in the spotlight from embarrassment, and it encourages group cooperation.

- ▲ If a player sings a line that doesn't connect to the theme, the group should find a way to bring it into the pattern.

▪ Reconvene the entire group and make the following comments:

- ▲ This exercise is not about performance, it is about participation and support. Timeliness and bravado are more important than musical talent. Jumping in often spurs an idea quicker than waiting on the sidelines.

- ▲ This type of activity is a great confidence builder because it tests your mind to see how it works under urgent conditions.

▪ Conclude the exercise by asking the group to brainstorm ways that having group support encourages individual players to take risks. You may write these ideas on an easel pad if you choose.

CAMERA!

The games reveal much about the obstacles that hinder learning. Through the improvisational lens, players see that by listening intently, working together, and accepting each others reality, there can be only success. You don't have time to think when you are looking out for another person.

GIBBERISH TRANSLATOR

 *Two players, speaking in gibberish, perform a task together. A third player translates so each player knows what is going on.*

GOALS

To enhance nonverbal aspects of speech.
To communicate in a playful way.
To experience the freedom of creation without having to justify the meaning of that creativity.
To work cooperatively on a joint project.

GROUP SIZE

Unlimited. 3 players at a time.

TIME

10–20 minutes.

PROCESS

▨ Introduce the game to the group as one in which they will be speaking gibberish. Define gibberish as the substitution of nonsense words and wordlike sounds for recognizable words, then demonstrate gibberish.

■ Have everyone in the group turn to a neighbor and begin speaking in gibberish. Encourage them to carry on a conversation rather than just mouthing sounds. Instruct them to converse as if each was making perfect sense. Allow duos to converse with other duos or individuals if they desire. The sole purpose is to have players experience speaking gibberish.

■ Allow this to continue for about 1 minute. Regain the groups attention and ask three volunteers to come forward.

■ Solicit a task or activity from the audience that the players will be engaged in. Limit the activities to ones that allow two people to converse with each other. Examples include making origami, building a dog house, or working on a jigsaw puzzle.

■ Using the volunteers as a demonstration team, give the following instructions:

▲ Decide among yourselves who will be Player 1, Player 2, and Player 3.

▲ Players 1 and 2, you are friends who have gotten together to work on a jigsaw puzzle (use the activity chosen by the group).

▲ While working on your activity, you will engage in conversation with each other. You can make statements, ask questions, or express feelings.

▲ The only thing different about this conversation is that it will be entirely in gibberish.

▲ Player 3 is the translator of the gibberish. Player 3, you will tell Player 1 what Player 2 has said and you will tell Player 2 what Player 1 has said. The conversation will continue back and forth between the two gibberish speakers through the translator.

▲ Players 1 and 2, ignore Player 3 but respond to what Player 3 tells you as you would if you had heard and understood the other player directly.

▲ Don't use recognizable words. Do use intonation, gestures, and inflection to convey meaning to the translator.

▲ Player 3, be quick and spontaneous with your translation. Watch the players as they speak and base your translation on your first impression or insight. You are totally fluent in the gibberish language so nothing said is beyond your ability to convey its meaning.

▪ Allow the players to practice the activity for 1–2 minutes for the benefit of the rest of the group. Players may sit or stand as they wish.

▪ Have the rest of the group form trios and allow them to determine who will be Player 1, 2, and 3 in each trio. Solicit a topic that everyone will use. The entire group will now participate in groups of three. When players are ready, have them begin using the new topic.

▪ Continue the gibberish game for 3–5 minutes, then regain everyone's attention and conclude with the following questions:

▲ Did the translator pass on what you communicated?

▲ Was fluency or continuity ever achieved? If so, under what conditions? If not, why not?

▲ Does this activity suggest that by paying close attention to intonation, gestures, and inflection, we might better communicate with one another?

VARIATIONS

▨ Have the activity be an instructional one where one player is teaching something to the other. Player 3 still is the translator. For example, instead of the two players each whittling a stick, Player 1 might be teaching Player 2 how to whittle.

▨ A more advanced version of gibberish translator is **Foreign movie** on page 48 of this book.

FOREIGN MOVIE

 *Using gestures and accented gibberish, players act out a scene which is ostensibly from a foreign movie. An equal number of other players translate the dialogue for the audience.*

GOALS

To develop teamwork by creating a team project through individual contributions that must be constantly melded into the overall team goal.

To enhance skills of listening and agreement.

GROUP SIZE

4 players at a time.

TIME

10 minutes.

PROCESS

▦ Introduce the goals of the exercise and ask for four volunteer players from the group. Bring the players to the stage and ask them to pair up. Ask each pair to decide who will be the actor and who will be the translator.

- Ask the audience for an example of a movie genre, such as film noir, gangster movie, western, or slapstick comedy. Genre is defined as a category characterized by a particular style, form, or content.

- Then ask the audience for an imaginary movie title they might like to see and ask for a language other than English. You may end up with something along the lines of a Polish horror film called "The Monster that Ate Warsaw." Provide the following comments to the audience:

  - During this activity, the actors are going to perform a scene totally in gibberish. Gibberish is unintelligible language where shaped sounds are substituted for recognizable words.

  - The translators will inform you what is happening.

- To begin the game, give the following instructions to the volunteer players on the stage:

  - Actors, use the audience suggestions to select the role each of you will play and the relationship your characters have to each other. For example, one of you may be the monster, the other may be the monster's kindergarten teacher, or each of you may be ordinary citizens waiting for the monster to come to their street.

  - Actors, inform the translators what have you have resolved. Do not let anyone else hear what you decided.

  - Actors, position yourselves on stage ready to begin a scene from the movie, mindful of the genre and language chosen. The game is called **Foreign movie**, so use gibberish with a foreign accent. Use physical motions and facial expressions to help communicate.

▲ Translators, position yourselves off to one side of the front of stage so you can see the action and still be heard and seen by the audience. Sit, stand, kneel, or crouch as you wish. Remember, you are watching and translating for only one of the actors.

▲ Translate each sentence, phrase, or idea of your actor. Whenever there is a pause in the actor's gibberish or action, decipher what has occurred and what's been said. Pay close attention to your actor so there isn't a lag between the action and the translation. Use your own experience with subtitles as a guideline for timing. Subtitles are used every couple of sentences to keep the story coherent for the viewer.

▲ Actors, listen carefully and respond to what the translators say. Allow the story to come out of the action and translation rather than from your predetermined ideas.

▲ Translators and actors, remain aware of what is going on in order to work together and keep the story going in a coherent way. This game works best when all participants are in sync with each other and when players are always ready to agree to what has been offered by other actors and translators.

▲ For example, our monster scene may open with Actor 1 as the monster, lumbering across the stage, stopping, then taking something from his pocket while spouting a sentence or two of Polish-accented gibberish. At the pause, Translator 1 says, "I hope this burger is still tasty. It's been two years since I bought it."

▲ Actor 1, it does not matter what you thought you were taking out of your pocket. You may have intended it to be a photograph. Once the translator has spoken, you and Actor 2 must agree with what has been translated.

▲ Use the translator's cue for your next action. Taste the burger! Speak in gibberish again and let the translator tell everyone the result. If the translation comes out "yummy," put a big smile on your face and pat your tummy. If the translation is "yuk," you may want to spit the burger out.

▲ Alternately, because you are in character as a monster, you may do the opposite of what is expected. A monster might find "yummy" as not good and "yuk" as delicious. You can make it up. Notice that whatever your choice, it is guided by your acceptance of the translation.

▲ During this activity, focus your attention on the action, plot development, and physical positions of the actors along with the story twists offered by the translators.

▲ Actors, do not speak when another is vocalizing.

▪ Continue the scene for approximately 3–5 minutes or until it reaches a natural ending point. Lead a closing discussion using the following questions:

▲ How could the skills and techniques employed here be useful in organizational and personal life?

▲ What was difficult about this exercise?

▲ What was easy about this exercise?

▲ Did any breakthroughs occur that made it easier as it went along?

▲ Did you discover anything about yourself that was especially interesting?

VARIATIONS

▨ Add another actor and another translator to make the scene more complex. This requires a heightened level of concentration and cooperation.

▨ **Foreign poet:** This variation uses the same structure with a poem instead of a movie as the art form. This version needs only two players.

▨ **Foreign commercial:** This exercise uses the same structure with a TV commercial as the medium for the actors. Instead of a genre, ask for a product that is sold in a foreign country.

MEMORY LOSS

 Player 1 tells a story but repeatedly pauses when a word or phrase is forgotten. Player 2 supplies a word or phrase, and Player 1 uses it to smoothly continue the story.

GOALS

To display confidence in the ability to adjust to whatever comes up.
To practice a high level of concentration.
To encourage players to activate their imagination.

GROUP SIZE

2 players at a time. Many duos can work simultaneously.

TIME

10–15 minutes.

PROCESS

▪ Bring two volunteer players to the stage. Allow them to decide who will be Player 1 and who Player 2.

▪ Introduce the game as one in which one player will tell a story for 2 minutes while the other player listens.

■ Solicit a topic for the players to use or allow the duos to choose their own.

■ Give the following instructions:

▲ Player 1, you will be the story teller. To demonstrate, I'd like you to talk about why you love your profession. After you begin talking, sporadically forget what you want to say: hesitate, repeat things, and say "ummm" a lot.

▲ Player 2, when Player 1 is at a loss for words, you must supply a word or brief phrase. Your word or phrase must be grammatically correct but need have no logical justification.

▲ It is generally not helpful for Player 2 to use articles, prepositions, or conjunctions.

▲ Player 1, repeat everything Player 2 says. Then add that information to your story in a way that continues to make sense. It is your responsibility to fit the suggestions into the story. The goal is to tell a complete story in the time allocated which is 2 minutes.

▲ Let's do a run through so you and the rest of the group can see how it works. After the run through, the entire group will pair off and play the game at the same time.

Give copies of the script that follows to Players 1 and 2.

▲ Player 1: "The reason I love my job is because um, um, um."

Player 2: "The money is so low."

Player 1: "The money is so low, and I am not tempted by materialism. This gives me a chance to um, um."

Player 2: "Whine."

Player 1: "Whine about the state of the company which is um, um."

Player 2: "Neolithic."

Player 1: "Neolithic. That means we work with our hands a lot which I love doing and that's why I love this job."

■ Make certain everyone has a partner. Solicit a topic for everyone to use or allow each duo to determine their own topic. Allow Player 1 in each duo to talk for 2 minutes. Signal the end of the segment and have the players switch roles. Allow Player 2 in each duo to speak for 2 minutes, then signal the end of the activity.

■ End the session with the following questions and discussion point:

▲ How are concentration and flexibility the keys to success in this game?

▲ Is Player 2 working with or against Player 1?

▲ Can you achieve a successful result without knowing exactly what that result will look like?

▲ When you have a goal such as finishing a story in mind, the outcome can be achieved even though you don't know what obstacles and detours lie in your way.

SHOPPING LIST

 Players learn to be flexible in their thought process while quickly responding to a series of objects in a logical conversation.

GOALS

To encourage flexible thinking.
To experience letting go of preconceived ideas.
To warm up a group.

GROUP SIZE

2 players at a time plus an emcee.

TIME

5–10 minutes. Don't go longer than 1–2 minutes with each round.

MATERIALS

Easel pad and markers or paper and pencil (only the emcee needs to have the list handy).

PROCESS

▨ Ask for two volunteers, Player 1 and Player 2, and bring them to the stage so that they are facing the audience.

▨ Before beginning the activity, ask the audience to compile a shopping list of ten to twenty items, explaining that a mixture of ordinary and unusual items, such as oatmeal, an umbrella stand, a bungee cord, and a shoe, works best for this exercise. Write the audience suggestions on the easel pad, then give the following instructions to the two players:

⏶ Decide which player will start the conversation.

⏶ In this activity, Player 1 and Player 2 will be engaged in a lively conversation. I will interrupt by calling out one of the items from my shopping list.

⏶ Player 1, when you hear the item, mention it within the conversation as quickly as possible. As soon as you mention the item, I will call out a second item.

⏶ Player 2, fit the second word into the ongoing conversation as soon as possible.

⏶ I will then call out a third item for Player 1 to use, and we'll continue through the list in the same manner.

⏶ Here's an example of how it might work using the examples I mentioned. Let's say the first word on the list is oatmeal.

Player 1: "I love eating oatmeal in the summer."

The second word on the list is umbrella stand.

Player 2: "I think oatmeal is very useful. Day old oatmeal makes an excellent umbrella stand."

The third word on the shopping list is bungee cord.

Player 1: "And it works great as a landing pad if your bungee cord breaks."

The next word is shoe.

Player 2: "I'll order take out for breakfast if you lend me a shoe."

Player 1: "Can I order oatmeal?"

▲ Don't search for the perfect answer. The key to this activity is in the fast connection to the word.

■ Continue in this manner until the list is completed or a predetermined time limit has been reached.

■ Lead a closing discussion with the following questions:

▲ Is it necessary to know the outcome of an activity in advance in order to be successful?

▲ By focusing on the immediate task (in this case the word of the moment), the solution to a problem unfolds one step at a time. How is this information relevant to solving a problem you are encountering in your daily life?

VARIATIONS

■ This game can be played by generating the shopping list using objects that are relevant to the players, the organization, or the industry.

■ The game can also be played in a "tag-team" approach, in which a new player replaces one of the original players after each new word is mentioned or with new duos for every round.

YOU TELL THE STORY

In this creative exercise, players learn to feel comfortable with uncertainty as they act out a scene guided only by audience suggestions.

GOALS

To be able to quickly and spontaneously change behavior.
To accept direction from others without hesitation or judgment.
To let go of the personal need to establish an outcome.

GROUP SIZE

2 players at a time and an emcee.

TIME

5–10 minutes.

PROCESS

■ Ask for two volunteers for the game. Ask the players to come to the stage. You will be the emcee when first introducing the game.

■ Ask audience members to determine who the characters on the stage are, what relationship they have to each other, and where the situation is taking place. (For example, they might be Olympic athletes from different countries in a locker room.) If desired, ask also for the first line of the scene.

■ Instruct the players to choose which character they will be and who will start. As emcee, give the following instructions:

▲ Players, start the scene when I say "begin" and continue the scene until I shout, "freeze!" at which time I would like you to stop action immediately while remaining frozen in the physical position.

▲ Next, emcee ask the audience to shout out what should happen next. It is important to remember that the responses may come in various ways depending on where the action is halted. Keep your questions appropriate to the scene. Ask questions that can be answered briefly. "Yes" or "no" questions are good. Avoid "why" questions. Examples of productive questions are: "Who's behind the door?" "Can he hear her?" "Does she believe him?" "Where was he for the past two years?" Examples of distracting questions are: "Why does she hate him?" "Why won't he leave?"

▲ Emcee, choose one of the answers, usually the first one heard, and repeat it loudly and clearly so the players and the audience know what was said.

▲ Players, then resume the scene in accordance with the audience's answer. You must incorporate the answer, no matter how unexpected it is. Remember to stay focused on the relationship of the characters in the scene. Remember, too, to use your body as much as possible. You can illustrate fear by screaming but you can also show it by being silent while shaking your entire body.

▲ Emcee, stay focused on the flow of the story. Be prepared to stop action at any time. Your role is particularly crucial as you dictate both the story and the pace of the game.

▦ After you finish giving the instructions, begin the scene and continue until it reaches a natural stopping spot, approximately 5 minutes.

▦ Lead a closing discussion using the following questions:

▲ What does this activity teach us about the ability to be flexible?

▲ Is there an advantage to having to respond without judgment, discussion, or hesitation?

▲ What is the most satisfying element of this game? What is the least satisfying?

VARIATIONS

▦ To make the game more interesting and more unpredictable, add a third or fourth person to the scene.

▦ For a slight variation of the exercise, the emcee may be either the facilitator or a member of the audience.

ONE WORD AT A TIME

 Players experience team identity by creating a unique story, one word at a time.

GOALS

To be in the moment at all times.

To let go of the need to figure out the ending or steer the outcome.

To experience trusting that the end result will be correct however it turns out.

GROUP SIZE

5–10 players at a time.

TIME

15 minutes.

PROCESS

■ Introduce the goals of the exercise to participants. Ask for five to ten volunteers and bring them to the stage. If there is an audience, arrange the players in a straight line, facing the audience. Otherwise, arrange them in a circle.

■ Introduce the game by telling the players they are going to create a story that's never been told before, and this story will be created one word at a time.

- Ask the observers in the room to select a title for the story the players are going to create. If there are no observers, the title can be chosen by the team of players.

- As titles are called out, choose the first title that you hear. As the director, by taking the first suggestion for the story title, you emphasize and model the importance of accepting whatever is offered, thereby demonstrating the law of agreement. If it's a real story such as "Goldilocks and the Three Bears," ask for elaboration on the story such as "Goldilocks Retires to Florida."

- Choose a player to begin and give the following instructions:

  - To create the story, each person will add one word at a time as the story progresses from one person to the next. After the first player says a word, the player to the right will add the second word. We will continue in this manner as each player contributes one word at a time to the story.

  - Remember to be spontaneous with your contribution. The most common block in this game is the desire to process what has gone before and to think about what to say.

  - It is important to stay focused on the story as a whole while remaining relaxed and ready for your turn.

  - When it is your turn to add a word, relate to the previous word in particular and the context of the story in general.

  - Do not anticipate the story before it arrives at your spot in the line and try not to get thrown by an unexpected word.

  - You cannot make a mistake because this story has never been told before so however it comes out is correct.

- As people stumble over their words and ideas, and the flow of the story is halted, feel free to start new stories. Explain to the players that starting over does not indicate failure.

- The storytellers may find it difficult to finish a sentence. When you begin to hear a string of clauses strung together with a chain of "ands," "therefores," and "howevers," remind the players that stories are made up of complete sentences. Encourage them to use voice inflection and tone to help determine when a sentence is over.

- Be prepared to start and stop several story titles before the group jells and completes a round.

- Continue until at least a partial story has been completed, which may be only be three or four sentences. It will be evident when the group has achieved spontaneity and flow.

- Lead a closing discussion by using the following questions:

  - What was easy or hard about this game?

  - When was the group successful?

  - When the story flowed smoothly, what happened to make it easier?

  - What insights did you learn about the game, yourself, and letting go of the end-result?

VARIATIONS

- This game can also be played with two people facing each other, each one offering one word at a time.

- In another variation, this game can be played with a large group divided into pairs. Each pair can have the same story title or each may have their own title.

THREE-HEADED EXPERT

 Three players representing one entity answer questions from the audience. They do this one word at a time.

GOALS

To integrate several improv skills.

To demonstrate the development of a team consciousness.

To sharpen listening skills.

To build confidence and trust among teammates.

GROUP SIZE

3 players at a time.

TIME

10–15 minutes.

PROCESS

This is an excellent structure for integrating many of the basic improv skills, so it works best after the group has experienced some of the other structures.

- Introduce the goals of the game and select three volunteers to be the players. Ask them to come to the stage and sit facing the audience.

- As you face the players, designate one player at either end as Player 1, the one in the middle as Player 2, and the one on the other end as Player 3. Turn to the audience and introduce the players.

  ▲ At this time I would like everyone to meet a "three-headed expert," the world's authority on everything.

  ▲ You may ask the expert any question you'd like an answer to. The question can be serious, such as "What is the solution to world hunger?" silly, such as "How can I find a parking spot when I need one?" or anything in-between.

  ▲ The expert will answer the question using all three heads. Each head will speak one word at a time, in sequence, starting with Player 1, proceeding to Player 2, on to Player 3, and continuing until the question is answered.

- After explaining the question process to the audience, provide the following instructions to the "three-headed expert:"

  ▲ Expert, do not hesitate, use more than one word at a time, or anticipate the outcome.

  ▲ Focus on the question to keep the answer relevant and recover quickly when the previous word tips you off balance.

  ▲ Listen carefully to your other heads. To be successful, focus on the previous words, the context of the question, and the intonation and inflection of the other players.

  ▲ Expert, when the answer is complete to your satisfaction, say in unison, "next question please." Any one head can decide when the question is answered, so listen carefully. When you hear "nnnee," jump in and in unison finish with "eext question please."

- After the above instructions have been given, begin the game by asking the audience to suggest a question for the expert.

- Continue the game for three or four questions from the audience, choose three new players, or lead a closing discussion using the following questions:

  ▲ When the process worked, why did it work?

  ▲ When it didn't work, why not?

VARIATIONS

- The game lends itself very well to the use of props. I sometimes use a large white bed sheet with three holes cut out for the experts' heads. The sheet hides the players' hands so they look more like a single person.

- Encourage the players to move as a single person, crossing their legs or gesturing with their hands together.

CONDUCTED STORY

 *Players collectively create something out of nothing by constructing a single, coherent story from short segments.*

GOALS

To promote team-building.
To develop a group mind by thinking within the same framework as teammates.
To practice being in the moment.

GROUP SIZE

4–6 players at a time plus a conductor.

TIME

10–20 minutes.

PROCESS

- Select four to six volunteers from the group.

- Bring the volunteers to the front of the room and arrange them in a semicircle, facing the audience. Explain that in this game the team will offer a story to the audience that's never been told before.

- Ask the audience to call out the name of a story they've never heard before but would like to hear now. Take any title suggestion the audience offers. There are no right or wrong answers.

- Choose the first suggestion you hear, repeat the title for the audience and team, then give the following instructions:

   ▲ We are going to create an impromptu story using the audience's suggestion. In this game, the story will be developed by a player, who will speak until signaled to stop.

   ▲ I will assume the role of conductor and orchestrate the creation of the story by pointing to one player at a time. The signal for you to start talking is when I point at you.

   ▲ First player, begin the story and continue until I point to someone else. First player, then immediately stop talking.

   ▲ Next player, pick up the story line from the precise place the last player stopped. If the previous player stopped in midsentence, finish the sentence. If the player stopped in midword, finish the word. You can take the story anywhere you like but you must pick up where it left off.

   ▲ When I point to someone else, the talking player will immediately stop and the next player will pick up the narration exactly at the point the previous player left off.

   ▲ The focal point is the story title. Use it as a guide if the story becomes chaotic or incomprehensible.

   ▲ Remember, there is no right or wrong way to do this activity. This story has never been told, so however it turns out is fine.

▲ Don't try to plan ahead as you wait for your turn. The story is likely to take some unexpected turns by the time it gets to you. Your attention needs to be on two things at all times; watching me and my movements and following the development of the story.

▲ Conclude the story at any time. Do this by using a recognized ending such as "they lived happily ever after," by referring to the title of the story such as, "and that's how Goldilocks retired to Hawaii," or by simply saying, "the end."

▲ The story works best when it is smooth and connected, rather than disjointed.

When you are ready to begin the story, assume a position facing the players. Stand, crouch, or sit in a chair as the conductor. A baton, stick, pencil, or other prop makes conducting more interesting and theatrical.

Begin the game by pointing at a player. Allow that player to narrate for about 30 seconds, then point to another player. Allow the second player about 30 seconds, then point to another. Make sure that each player has a turn before you give any player a second turn.

After the first go around, move more quickly between players. Jump around with your choices, choosing players randomly. This keeps them alert and focused on you and the story at the same time.

If the players are completely out of sync with each other, stop the action, get another title, and start again.

Continue until a story conclusion has been reached or you

decide to stop the game. Bring up another team of volunteers if time allows.

▦ Lead a closing discussion using the following questions:

▲ What elements make a story interesting? (action, characters, conflict, resolution, and attention to environment)

▲ Was it frustrating being unable to stay with the story line you had in your mind?

▲ When it was another player's turn, how did you manage to keep your attention on the story and away from what you planned to say?

VARIATIONS

▦ Repeat the exercise but allow an audience member or a team player to conduct the exercise.

▦ Choose a story topic specifically related to the company, organization, group, or topic you are working with. (For example, how ABC Company became the best in its business or secrets of successful communication.)

▦ **Story, story, die:** A competitive form of **Conducted story.** If a player flubs a transition, the conductor or any audience member yells out "die" and that competitor is out. Flubbing may be defined as stammering, using the previous player's last word as your first word, ignoring the transition word, or other guidelines determined ahead of time by the group. The "dead" player then exits the game by leaving the stage or by dramatically falling to the floor and remaining there until the game is finished. Other players close ranks. Continue the game until only one player is left. When that happens, the last player quickly wraps up the story.

SOAPBOX SYMPHONY

 *This is an excellent activity to improve players' listening and multitasking skills as they role play a "spokesperson" for a particular gripe or source of anger. Together, the team produces a symphony of strong emotions.*

GOALS

To experience team identity.
To build comfort with spontaneity.
To offer an outlet for releasing frustration.

GROUP SIZE

4–6 players at a time plus a conductor.

TIME

10–20 minutes.

PROCESS

▪ Introduce the exercise goals to the group and select four to six volunteers to be players of the game. Bring the players to the front of the room and arrange them in a semicircle facing the audience.

- Begin the game by asking the audience to reveal a topic they feel angry or frustrated about. This may be a personal annoyance, such as the frustration of always getting into the slowest line at the bank, or a more global exasperation, such as the inequities in the tax system.

- Obtain as many different topics as you have players. Write the topics on a piece of paper to remember them.

- When enough topics have been collected, ask a player to step forward and proceed with the following instruction:

  ▲ Player 1 (use the name of the player being pointed to, for example, Peter) told me earlier today how much he hates (put in one audience suggestion here, for example, always getting into the slowest line). Peter, tell us what bothers you about being in slow lines. Speak spontaneously and enthusiastically about the subject for 30 seconds. I will signal when you should stop. Ready? Begin.

- After approximately 30 seconds, signal Player 1 to stop, thank Player 1, then move on to Player 2. Assign a second topic from the list to Player 2. Allow Player 2 to expound for 30 seconds, then continue this process until each of the players has had a chance to present a different frustration.

- After each player has spoken, arrange them in a line and assume an orchestra conductor's position facing them. You may choose to stand, crouch, or sit in a chair. A baton, stick, pencil, or other prop makes conducting more interesting and theatrical.

- Give the following instructions:

- Imagine that I am the conductor and you are the orchestra. Your voices are your instruments. I am going to lead this symphony of emotion by pointing to you, the players.

- When I point at you, I would like you to begin to spontaneously talk about your previous topic with an attitude of anger, frustration, exasperation, or whatever is appropriate. Pretend you are making a speech to a crowd of supporters.

- You will need to speak to the audience while keeping an eye on me. Continue speaking until I signal you to stop or point to another player.

- The object is to keep your exposition going as smoothly as possible. When your turn comes, pick up your argument from where you left off the last time. To keep things flowing, try to use the previous players ending as a smooth transition into your turn.

- Remember to speak spontaneously, even if you repeat things you've already said. It is better to repeat statements over again than to stumble and go "uh-uh."

- As the conductor, I will control the volume and tempo with my hands. When I move my hands faster, pick up the pace of your speech. When my hands move slower, slow your pace down. When I want you to speak louder, I will raise my hands as a conductor would. When I lower my hands, lower the volume.

- In an orchestra, instruments play together, therefore I may activate two or more players at the same time. If I want you to continue while another player is talking, I'll use the universal come-here signal by waving my hand towards me.

▲ When more than one player is talking, I may want one to be loud, another to be soft at the same time. Watch my hands to see how to respond. Let's begin.

▪ Begin the game by pointing to one of the players.

▪ Complete the symphony in a powerful and exciting way by having all players end suddenly and in unison. Here is the process to accomplish that climax.

  ▲ Bring all the voices into play, one at a time where each player is speaking at top volume about their own subject. Every player will be speaking at the same time. It will likely be impossible to understand the individual arguments.

  ▲ Once all the players are actively speaking, establish and maintain eye contact with them all. Begin to raise the volume by indicating so with the baton or your hands. Move directly in front of those who don't see you. Having every player aware of you is crucial here.

  ▲ When you have everyone's attention and the volume is high, slowly bring your hands up over your head, wave your hands to indicate you want the players to continue at this level, then drop your hands down quickly. The players will end at the same time, creating a rush of silence that will quickly be filled with cheers and applause from the audience and smiles from the players.

▪ Lead a closing discussion using the following questions:

  ▲ What are the obstacles to success in this game?

  ▲ Why do people like to watch this game?

  ▲ Why do they like to participate?

▲ Notice how well we can present someone else's argument. Why is that? Does this suggest that we have many things in common with other people? How could you use this insight in your daily life?

SCULPTING

In this creative exercise, one player is "sculpted" to resemble the physical appearance of another player, helping participants explore life from a different perspective.

GOALS

To see the world from a different point of view.

To understand one's self better.

To experience how physical stance affects outlook, emotion, and perception of a person.

GROUP SIZE

Unlimited.

TIME

15–25 minutes.

PROCESS

▦ Introduce the exercise goals and form groups of three participants. Describe the activity as a way of looking at ourselves and

others through new and different eyes. Provide the following instructions:

- At this time I would like each trio to identify the members of your group as players A, B, and C. Players A and B, stand side by side, facing in the same direction. Stand in a natural and relaxed manner, looking out in the distance.

- Player C, you are going to be the sculptor. I want you to use Player A as a model and Player B as the clay.

- Player C, begin to mold Player B into as close a replica of Player A as possible by physically adjusting Player B's body.

- While Player C is sculpting Player B, I want Player A to remain very still and relaxed.

- Player B, stay loose while allowing Player C to manipulate your body. Keep the poses you are placed into.

- Player C, continually refine the molding so that Players A and B look as similar as possible, down to the smallest detail. Consider particulars such as the tilt of the head, the position of the feet, the bearing of the torso, and the demeanor of the facial features.

- You may ask other group members to help you refine your work since they will see things you may not. You will have 5 minutes for this sculpting process. I will signal you when time is up.

◼ After 5 minutes, call time and give the following instructions to the A Players:

- I would like Player A in each trio to step out now and look at Player B who will remain in position.

▲ Player A, think about what you see and reflect on how it feels to look at yourself. Ask yourself these questions:

Who is that person?

What can I learn from looking at this sculpture?

▲ As you think about these questions, you may write your thoughts down on paper when this activity is over or keep them in your head to reflect on later.

▲ Now I would like Player B in each trio, still in the body stance as Player A, to consider what it's like to be this other person.

What do you know of them?

What does it feel like to be this person?

What did you learn from feeling the world as this person that you couldn't know from just looking at Player A?

Where is the center of this person?

What is this person's source of strength?

What does this person feel like doing right now?

▲ As you think about these questions, you may write your thoughts down on paper when this activity is over or keep them in your head to reflect on later.

■ Reconvene the entire group and lead a closing discussion by asking participants to share any insights they gained during this activity.

VARIATION

■ If time permits, allow players to switch roles.

LEAD WITH YOUR BODY

Players stroll around the room and discover the "character" within themselves as they learn to overcome their feelings of self-consciousness.

GOALS

To practice different ways of seeing and experiencing the world. To locate a "character" within each player.

GROUP SIZE

Unlimited.

TIME

10 minutes.

> *Make sure space is adequate for players to move around the room comfortably without bumping into each other.*

PROCESS

▪ Introduce the goals of the game, then ask participants to stand up where they are. Give them the following instructions:

▲ At this time I would like everyone to stroll around the room in a natural and relaxed way using any pattern you desire.

▲ Don't look around to see what other people are doing. It's not unusual to feel foolish or self-conscious. Acknowledge it, then let it go. Stay in the moment and keep strolling.

▨ After 30 seconds, give the following instructions:

▲ Focus your attention on a specific part of your body. It may be an external part such as an arm, foot, or ear, or it may be an internal part such as your heart or brain or an eardrum or white blood cell.

▲ Let that body part lead your walk as if it were the first part of your body that would walk into anything.

▲ Continue to walk with the leading body part out front for 45–60 seconds. Keep your focus on your own body, not on what others are doing.

▨ When everyone has established this walk, give the following instructions:

▲ Add gibberish sounds to go along with your movement. You will then be walking around with a physical posture other than your usual one and uttering nonsense words.

▲ Continue to stay focused on the body part that is leading your walk. Listen to the rhythm of the sounds tumbling from your mouth.

▲ Consider now, based on your physical movement and your sounds, who you are in this body. Where are you coming from? Where might you be going?

▲ Live and move in this new person's life until I yell, "freeze!"

■ Allow participants to continue walking for approximately 45 seconds and then shout "freeze!" Ask players to experience the world through this character's eyes for a few moments.

■ Instruct participants to return to their chairs and lead a discussion using the following comments and questions:

▲ As each of you were strolling around the room, your actions and your acceptance of what was offered created a character, one with a personality and a purpose.

▲ Many different feelings may have arisen as you were in character. What were some of these feelings? What part of your body did the feelings come from?

▲ Did the change in body carriage cause a change in your view of the world? If so, in what way?

▲ How would you have proceeded if I had started this exercise by simply asking you to create a character?

■ Close the session with the following statement:

▲ We all have characters within us who come alive from body cues, not mind-sets. By creating a character and giving that character a reason to be, you create reality. This is why when you see someone on a bus, in a line, or crossing the street, you can construct an entire existence for that person just from the way they carry themselves in any one moment.

VARIATION

■ Allow players while still in character to interact with other characters. Encourage them to ask each other simple, direct questions such as: Where are you going? What's the weather going to be like tomorrow? Would you like to see a picture of my baby?

THIS IS NOT A ROPE

 *Each player uses a piece of rope in a way that converts the rope into something else.*

GOALS

To see things from a different perspective.
To find new ways of looking at familiar objects.
To encourage risk taking.

GROUP SIZE

5–15 players.

TIME

10–20 minutes.

MATERIALS

A three- to four-foot-long rope.

PROCESS

▦ Arrange the group in a circle or a straight line. With a large group, you may set up several circles. Have a rope for each subgroup.

■ Introduce the game as one in which the rope will be transformed by each player into something other than what it is.

■ Give the following instructions:

▲ When it is your turn, step forward, take the rope and say, "This is not a rope, it is a . . . ." As you name it, demonstrate its new use. For example, you might say, "This is not a rope, it is a snake." Get down on the floor and slither the rope around as if it were a snake.

▲ However, it doesn't have to be a snake. You might just as easily say, "It is a picture frame." Then, make a loop with the rope and put your face through it.

▲ When you are through with your transmutation of the object, place it on the floor and return to your space.

▲ Any other player then immediately steps in, picks up the rope and says, "This is not a rope, it is a . . . ." Player 2 then demonstrates what the rope has become.

▲ We will continue until everyone has had three opportunities to work with the rope. If two players reach for the rope at the same time, preference goes to the player who hasn't yet participated. If both players have already participated, the more recent player steps back.

■ Place the rope on floor in the center of the circle or in front of the line. Start the game by allowing any player who is ready to pick up the rope.

■ Having players work with the rope three times allows for deeper exploration into what the rope can become. When players get stuck, have them put the rope into motion of some kind. Throwing it, waving it, or rolling it will suggest ideas to the stuck player. Keep a list of many uses for the rope. This will enable you to ask questions that will jump-start players who get stuck.

■ Continue until all players who want to participate have done so or until time is up.

■ Conclude with the following questions:

▲ What factors lead to success in this game?

▲ As kids, we all showed the ability to transform everyday objects into many things. Why don't we do so as adults?

▲ What happens to our spontaneity and creativity as we get older? How can we avoid losing them?

▲ How does the movement of the object help us see new possibilities for its use?

VARIATION

■ Use an object other than a rope. Suggestions include a stick, a roll of toilet paper, a baking pan, or a videocassette.

FREEZE TAG

Players learn the importance of team dynamics in this playful exercise, which allows them to create reality using information from the body and emotions rather than thought.

GOALS

To trust team members.
To build team rapport.
To increase confidence.

GROUP SIZE

Works best with 5–10 people on a team. Several teams can play at the same time.

TIME

10–20 minutes.

PROCESS

▢   Introduce the goals of the exercise and arrange the group in a circle if everyone is participating or in a semicircle if there is an audience.

■ Select two volunteer players and ask them to step forward or move to the middle of the circle. The rest of the team will watch and be ready to participate.

■ Give the following instructions to the first two players:

▲ Begin to move or stretch any way you choose. You can wave your arms, hop around, comb your hair, or move however you want as long as you are in motion in some manner.

▲ After a few seconds, I will loudly shout "freeze!" and at that time, both players will immediately freeze.

▲ Next the audience will tell us who these characters on stage are, where they are, and what relationship they have to each other. For example, they may be first graders on the first day of school in the cafeteria.

▲ Using the audience suggestion, either player will now begin the scene. Use your body position as the source for inspiration. For example, if Player 1 is on his knees, he may say, "Boy, the food on this school floor is delicious," as he puts fingers into his mouth. If his hands had been in the air, he may say, "I can see what I want on top of the counter, but I can't get to it. I'll climb on the back of this other kid."

▲ Player 2, use the information Player 1 gives and continue the same scene. If Player 1 is on the floor, drop down and say, "I'll trade you this old gum I found on the floor for that cookie crumb." If Player 1 talks about climbing on your back, let him do it and continue the scene.

▲ Always agree to what other players offer. If your partner offers to trade his old gum for your cookie, don't block by replying, "That's not gum in your hand."

▲ Continue the scene until another player, Player 3, not presently in the episode, yells "freeze!" That person can be anyone in the circle. This may happen at any time and should happen at least every couple of minutes.

▲ Player 3, enter the arena and tap one of the other two players on the back. Assume the exact physical position of the tapped player. The exiting player will not leave the space until the new player has physically moved into the space.

▲ Player 3 will begin a new scene that must evolve from the current physical position of the players. Always begin by making a statement or taking a positive action. For example, if you are in a stance with your finger pointing towards a wall, say, "Look at that enormous two-headed buffalo," rather than "What is that over there?" The opening line of the new scene must make the situation the players are in clear so the new scene is immediately understood.

▲ Continue the scene until someone else yells "freeze!" and enters the action.

▲ Listen to your body for insight into the reality of the situation you are creating.

▲ Listen to your partner with your eyes, ears, and body to keep the scene alive, moving, and interesting. Remember to keep in motion. There will be a tendency to stand still while exchanging words.

▲ Keep from stepping on each others' lines by remembering to listen. Respond to what the other person is saying or doing. Don't talk at the same time as another player.

▲ Players, yell "freeze" loudly and enthusiastically when you are ready to enter. You may also clap your hands at the same time for emphasis. Come into the scene with purpose, energy, and commitment. Do not stroll in nonchalantly. The player coming in will take the place of a person who was in the scene.

- Players can jump in at any time. When you see players floundering, the best thing you can do is get them off the hook. You would want them to do the same for you. Take risks and jump in without being certain of what you will say. Experience shows that an idea you develop while waiting on the sidelines will usually not fit by the time you get into the action.

- Before jumping in, allow the scene to unfold just long enough to establish the relationship between the players.

- It is as important for observing players to attend to the action as it is for the players in the scene to be focused and involved at all times.

- You don't have to wait until everyone has a turn before jumping in again.

- Continue until time is up or everyone who wants to has had a chance to participate.

- Reconvene the entire group and lead a closing discussion using the following questions:

  - How does this game build trust and rapport among players?

  - What were the feelings of vulnerability and riskiness you experienced in this game?

  - How did you feel when you were on the sidelines waiting to come in?

▲ Were you more comfortable on the sidelines or in the action?

VARIATION

▓ **Object tag:** Players start with an object that they must use in the scene. Every time a new player enters, the object must change identity and somehow be used. The object can never be used for what it really is. Any object will do—hat, cup, ball, marker, etc. For example, Player 1 offers a pencil as a trophy to Player 2 for outstanding service. The scene continues until Player 1 is replaced by Player 3 whose first line is, "Be careful of that laser gun. I lost a partner that way." The scene continues until Player 4 replaces Player 2 and describes the pencil as a pound of dehydrated spaghetti.

ACTION!

Improv works best when there is movement and action. Take the risk, say the word off the top of your head, and let your body go into motion. Encourage the players to show rather than describe what is going on. Improv is like skiing—take the action and the brain aligns with what is happening.

MISSION IMPOSSIBLE

 This fast-paced exercise encourages participants to find as many creative new uses for an object as possible.

GOALS
To encourage "out-of-the-box thinking."
To experience making unusual choices.
To fight the desire to see things in the context of "it's always been this way."

GROUP SIZE
Unlimited.

TIME
10–20 minutes.

MATERIALS
Paper; pens or pencils; easel pad and markers.

PROCESS

The following is one possible setup for the game. It uses a paper clip as the source for creativity. Naturally, you can design names, missions, and objects as needed.

▪ Introduce the exercise to the group and form groups of five to eight participants if possible.

▪ Explain to the group that this activity is an exercise in brainstorming. Provide the following tips on effective brainstorming:

- ▴ Creativity consultant Mel Donaghue offers the acronym "dove" as a way to remember the basics for brainstorming:

  D—Don't judge the ideas

  O—Outrageous ideas are desirable

  V—Volume and Variety in ideas are needed

  E—Extend and Elaborate on ideas presented earlier in the game

▪ Give participants the following instructions:

- ▴ Let's imagine that your group works for the Impossible Mission Force and has been called in to ACME Paper Clip Company on assignment. ACME has just learned that a company overseas recently developed an item that makes paper clips obsolete. In order to survive, ACME needs to develop new, practical uses for the paper clip.

- ▴ I am going to give each group a piece of paper and a pencil. Please select a recorder to write down the group's ideas.

- ▴ For the next 5 minutes, I would like each group to generate as many uses for a paper clip as you can. Don't judge your ideas. Remember, this is an uninhibited brainstorming session. Recorders, write all the ideas down on paper so they can be shared with the entire group later.

▲ Now, focus on the paper clip and its new possibilities. Immediately discard negative or blocking thoughts.

▲ Don't judge the value or practicality of your ideas, just toss them out randomly.

■ After the brainstorming session, reconvene the entire group and ask the recorders to read aloud their groups' creative new ideas for the paper clip. You may record them all on an easel pad if you wish.

■ After reflecting on these new uses for the paper clip, lead a closing discussion using the following questions:

▲ During this brainstorming session, did you encounter any blocks to your creativity?

▲ What behaviors helped you overcome these problems?

▲ What was the most helpful insight you learned?

▲ Did the creative process change for you as the game progressed? In what way?

▲ How does working in a group help or hinder brainstorming?

VARIATIONS

■ To vary this activity, use any unfamiliar object as the brainstorming source.

■ To make the exercise more practical for everyday life, use a relevant conceptual problem such as "how to help employees deal with organizational changes" as the brainstorming objective. Remember to adhere to the brainstorming rules even with relevant problems.

JUMP EMOTION

 Players learn the importance of accepting and agreeing with others as two players act out a scenario using emotions which are manipulated by an emcee.

GOALS
To stay in the moment.
To unconditionally accept and agree to what is offered by another.

GROUP SIZE
2 at a time plus an emcee.

TIME
10 minutes.

PROCESS
▪ Introduce the goals of the exercise, then select two volunteers from the group. Bring the two players to the stage.

▪ Elicit a list of at least ten emotions from the audience and write them on a piece of paper or easel pad. It doesn't matter whether the list of emotions is seen by the audience.

▣ After collecting the list of emotions, ask the audience to determine the characters' roles, their relationship to each other, and where the situation is taking place. (For example, high school sweethearts who haven't seen each other in twenty-five years meet at their high school reunion.)

▣ Ask the players to determine who will be Player 1 and who will be Player 2, then provide the following instructions:

▴ When I tell you to start, Player 1, begin a conversation based on the audience's suggestion. Remember to stay in character. I will allow the conversation to develop for a few sentences and will then shout out one of the emotions from the list we generated earlier.

▴ As soon as an emotion is announced, Player 1, immediately adopt the specified emotion as the tone for your conversation. Both players, continue using the same emotion until the next changeover. The quicker the changeover, the better. Quick reversals of emotion are most enjoyable for the audience.

▴ For example, if happiness is the specified emotion, the scene might read like this. Player 1 is speaking and after a few sentences says, "I'm so thrilled to see you after all these years. This makes my whole trip here worthwhile."

▴ At this point, I call out the listed emotion "rage."

▴ Player 1, continue the conversation but adopt the new emotion. "And I'm furious you made me so happy. You didn't even notice me, and I've been waiting for you for twenty-five long years. You ruined my entire day."

▴ Player 2 respond with whatever statement you like, but clothe it in rage. "I was just getting something to eat, and you had to come over. Excuse me while I go and punch the wall."

- ▲ At this point, I call out the listed emotion "confusion."

- ▲ Player 2 say, "By the way, who are you?"

- ▲ Player 1, because we're still in confusion answers, "I'm not sure I understand your question. I'm Artie, your first love."

- ▲ Continue the action and conversation until it reaches a natural end point, such as one character exiting the scene to go to the bathroom, or I will step in and say "cut."

- ▲ Listen carefully during the scene to each other so you respond to what your partner says and does rather than what you think should happen.

- ▲ Make the scene come alive by adding movement to the conversation, using your whole body to show the emotion.

- ▲ Show emotions with actions as well as words. Silent crying and wiping tears away is more effective than saying "I'm sad."

▨ After the instructions are finished, begin the exercise. Continue the scene until it reaches a natural stopping spot, time runs out, or all the emotions are utilized.

▨ If time permits, bring another pair up to act out the role play. Gather new emotions for each pair.

▨ When the predetermined time is reached, lead a closing discussion using the following questions:

- ▲ Does everyone treat a specific emotion in the same way?

- ▲ Would it be helpful to use the technique of changing emotions in everyday conversations or arguments? Why or why not?

VARIATION

Jump style: This variation uses film, theater, and literary genres in place of emotions. The emcee collects and calls out different styles for players to use. Genres include mystery, western, soap opera, and musical.

IT'S TUESDAY

 Players perform short scenarios using the previous player's last line as their first.

GOALS
To practice spontaneity.
To constructively use whatever is offered by a team member.
To experience how emotion affects communication.

GROUP SIZE
3–15 players.

TIME
10–20 minutes.

PROCESS
▣ Arrange the group in a circle.

▣ Ask for a topic of conversation from the group. Accept the first one you hear. For illustrative purposes, let's use reengineering for our topic.

▣ Give the following instructions:

⏶ This game is called **It's Tuesday**. Each of us will have the opportunity to speak spontaneously for approximately half a minute. Your topic will be determined by the player before you.

⏶ You will step into the circle and begin your spontaneous speech full of force and emotion. You will moderate your emotional intensity and volume during the course of your turn until you end your speech calmly and gently by using a benign, neutral phrase. When you are done, step back, and the player to your left will take over.

⏶ Using the topic word "reengineering" as an example, the first round may sound like this: (loudly and emotionally) "Reengineering is the hardest thing to swallow in this company. People work all their lives to get to a certain place in the company, and all of a sudden they are reengineered into a new career. I'm going to talk to somebody about this! (less fury, more gently) But I really can't do it today. I have to get my shoes shined. I have to look good. After all, it's Tuesday."

⏶ Notice that by the end of my scenario, I was very calm. It's Tuesday is almost an afterthought.

⏶ Now that I've finished, I will step back and the next player, Player 1, steps forward and uses my final phrase or sentence to begin a new spontaneous speech on a completely different subject.

⏶ Player 1, take my final phrase and use it with high emotion.

Hand a copy of the following paragraphs to Players 1 and 2 so they can read the examples.

Player 1: "It's Tuesday! Oh no! They are going to repossess my car today. I've got to find $300 by noon or I'm sunk. Why did

I ever go to Vegas with that money. (Less anger, more gently) I don't even like neon lights. Nothing went right. Bad food, bad weather. Even the hotel was a disaster. The towels weren't very fluffy."

▲ Player 2: "The towels weren't very fluffy! Did I hear you correctly? You expect to be hired as our national sales manager because you like to take showers in hotels? (Less anger, gently) That's the most original approach to getting a job I've ever heard. I'll let you know tomorrow. Right now, I need a nap."

▲ Player 3 will start off with "Right now, I need a nap" at a high level of intensity and emotion.

▪ After concluding the sample round, decide who will begin the game and elicit a topic or phrase from the group. Continue the game until everyone has had a turn or time runs out.

▪ Conclude the activity with the following questions:

▲ Emotions play an important part in communication. How does emotional context determine the effect our words have on listeners?

▲ It is often easier to be involved in an event than to be observing it. As you were observing, how did you feel watching others be spontaneous?

▲ Did the fact that you had no control over what phrase you would be forced to use make the game easier or harder?

VARIATION

▪ Allow any player to jump in rather than going in a particular order.

WHAT ARE YOU DOING?

 *Players learn to focus on what is actually happening rather than what is being said.*

GOALS
To separate action from discussion.
To allow mind and body to operate separately.

GROUP SIZE
2 players at a time.

TIME
5–10 minutes.

PROCESS
▦ Introduce the goals of the exercise to participants. Select two players from the group and bring them to the stage.

▦ Describe the game as a combination of contradictory words and actions.

▦ Determine who will be Player 1 and who will be Player 2. Provide the following instructions to the two players:

- Player 1 will mimic a physical action, such as writing a letter, while Player 2 asks, "What are you doing?" Player 1 responds by naming some other activity, such as "I'm washing the car." Player 2 then acts out washing a car. Let's begin.

- Player 1, begin to pantomime a physical action, such as bouncing a ball.

- Player 2, after Player 1 starts the action, say "What are you doing?"

- Player 1, continue the action but answer the question by naming an activity different from what you are actually doing. For example, "I'm brushing my teeth."

- Player 2, immediately begin miming the action Player 1 stated, not the activity Player 1 is doing. In this case, begin brushing your teeth.

- Player 1, it is now your turn to ask, "What are you doing?"

- Player 2, respond with something other than "brushing my teeth" such as "I'm digging a ditch."

- Player 1, act out digging a ditch as Player 2 asks, "What are you doing?"

- Player 1, answer with an activity other than digging a ditch such as, "I'm reading a book."

- The objective is to answer smoothly and without hesitation. The round continues until one player takes too long to answer, stutters, or otherwise flubs a response, answers with the actual activity being pantomimed, or repeats an answer.

- The audience will determine when a player is removed by an agreed upon method such as shouting "out."

- A player who is "out" leaves the stage and is quickly replaced by another volunteer player.

- The player who remains becomes Player 1 and starts a new action.

- Quick responses are necessary. The secret to success is to separate thought from action. You can act by just moving a body part. A tongue wiggle or hand twitch is fine. Remember, you don't have to explain what it is. To answer the question, "What are you doing?" look around the room (I'm sitting in a chair; I'm holding a pencil; I'm writing on a flip chart) or think about something in your past (I'm getting my diploma; I'm proposing marriage).

After a predetermined time limit is reached, reconvene the group and lead a closing discussion using the following questions:

- What made this game fun?

- What made it easy for you to volunteer?

- What made it difficult for you to volunteer?

- What happens in an organization or relationship when what is said is not in alignment with what is being done?

VARIATION

The game can be played with a group arranged in a circle or line. Player 1 starts the action, and Player 2 asks, "What are you doing?" Player 1 responds. Player 2 turns to Player 3 and acts out Player 1's response. Player 3 asks, "What are you doing?" and so on until everyone has had a chance or time is up.

3 THINGS IN 3 MINUTES

 Two players at a time work on improving their listening skills and becoming comfortable with taking directions from another person.

GOALS

To put yourself totally under another person's direction.
To practice agreement and listening skills.

GROUP SIZE

2 players at a time plus a timekeeper.

TIME

5–10 minutes per pair.

PROCESS

▪ Select two volunteers and ask them to come to the stage. Have the players determine who will leave and who will stay, then give the following instructions:

  ▲ Player 1, leave the room so you can't hear what's going on in here. Someone will come to get you when we are ready.

- Audience, now that Player 1 can't hear us, we are going to decide on three things we would like Player 1 to do upon returning. For example, we may want Player 1 to sneeze, roar like a lion, and take a nap.

- Player 2, you will have 3 minutes to get Player 1 to do the three predetermined things. You will not be able to tell Player 1 directly what to do. You must imply, suggest, and hint.

- To get Player 1 to sneeze, for example, you might say, "You look like you have a cold." She may blow her nose, which is a good guess but not the right answer.

- Continue with, "Didn't you tell me you once had allergies?"

- When Player 1 sneezes, the audience will applaud and cheer so the players will know they got it right.

- Player 2 will move quickly to the next action, asking, for example, "What's your sign?'

- Player 1 might reply, "Taurus" and begin acting like a bull.

- Player 2 now continues with "I had you pegged as a perfect Leo."

- Player 1 will roar like a lion, and the audience will applaud.

- Player 2 says, "I wish we were in kindergarten again."

- Player 1 will begin to skip.

- Player 2 will say "My favorite part was right after snack time. I wish I had my old blanket back."

- Player 1 will drop to the floor and starts to snore. Audience will respond loudly.

■ After the above instructions are given, begin the exercise. Ask the audience for three actions for Player 1 to perform. Call Player 1 back into the room and give these additional instructions:

▲ We've come up with three things we'd like you to act out for us. Player 2 will allude to them but won't tell you what the three things are.

▲ The best way for you accomplish this task is to act rather than to think. Listen for the clues, then act out quickly.

▲ If Player 2 asks if you have a cold, you may sneeze, cough, blow your nose, or make another action that you connect with having a cold. If you hit on one of the desired actions, we will applaud and cheer you. Player 2 has 3 minutes to get you to perform the three actions.

▲ Player 2, suggest the actions in any order you choose.

▲ Audience, you may boo if you feel that any clue is too obvious or direct.

■ Choose a timekeeper and begin the exercise.

■ Lead a closing discussion using the following questions:

▲ How can we balance the need to listen carefully with the drive for immediate and quick action?

▲ What negative consequences can occur when we act without knowing exactly what needs to be done?

▲ What positive consequences can occur when we act without knowing exactly what needs to be done?

VARIATION

■ **Pop:** Present an interesting place, occupation, and physical characteristic for Player 2 to act out.

LIMERICK

 Players tell a story in the form of a limerick with each player, in turn, suppling one line of the limerick until it is done.

GOALS

To share in the creation of something new in an ensemble manner.
To be part of a creative team.
To contribute to a design where personal contribution is not as important as group effort.

GROUP SIZE

5 players at a time.

TIME

5–10 minutes.

PROCESS

▪ Explain that a team of players is going to create and present a brand new limerick to the group.

▪ Before the exercise begins, define a limerick as a light or humorous verse of five lines written in the rhyme scheme A, A, B, B, A. Lines two and five rhyme and share meter with line one. Lines three and four rhyme and share meter with each other. For example:

There once was a guy from the moon.
Whose birthday was the 30th of June.
He was a man with no hair.
And he'd never breathed air.
But, boy, could he carry a tune.

■ Select five volunteer players to come to the stage. Ask them to stand in a row facing the audience.

■ While you are facing the players, assign the first player on your left number 1, the next player 2, and so on until all five of the players have a number. Provide the following instructions:

▲ As a team, you will create a limerick which you know is a five line verse whose rhyme scheme is A, A, B, B, A. Let me remind you of the format by reading the example limerick (or another one of your choosing) again.

▲ Player 1, begin with a first line, a line you make up using the limerick format.

▲ Player 2, contribute the next line, using the same meter and rhyme as Player 1.

▲ Player 3, contribute the third line which should not rhyme with either line one or line two.

▲ Player 4, contribute the next line using the same meter and rhyme as Player 3.

▲ Player 5, contribute the last line using the same meter and rhyme as Players 1 and 2.

> ▲ Players, keep in mind the type of line you must contribute and the context of the limerick as it develops.

■ After the first team of volunteers is finished, select a new team of five for another limerick if time allows.

■ Lead a closing discussion using the following questions:

> ▲ How did you feel when you were playing the game?

> ▲ How did you make decisions about what to do when your turn came up?

> ▲ Have you ever composed a limerick before? Could you do it in the future?

VARIATIONS

■ Ask the audience for a subject for the limerick or a word to end the first line with.

■ Rather than proceeding sequentially, allow players to jump in randomly to complete the next line.

■ To add variety, ask players to improvise a blues song instead of a limerick. The blues variation works especially well when a player or the facilitator plays a guitar or harmonica.

YES, AND . . .

 Participants learn the importance of agreement and improve their listening skills through the use of role playing.

GOALS
To foster cooperation.
To improve interpersonal relationships and listening skills.
To demonstrate the basic improv principal that "agreement is the one rule that can never be broken."

GROUP SIZE
2 players per scene.

TIME
3–5 minutes per scene.

PROCESS
▧ Introduce the structure as a game in which each player must agree with the others no matter what is said.

▧ Present the following example:

- Player 1 should start a conversation with a positive, declarative statement.

- Player 2 agrees with Player 1 by first saying "Yes and . . . ," then making her own declarative statement. Thus, after responding positively, you carry the conversation and the story forward by adding to the information.

- If Player 1 says, "Let's go to the movies," Player 2 might answer "Yes, and let's sneak some popcorn into the theater." Player 1 says, "Yes, and I'll put the butter in my pocket." Player 2 responds, "Yes, and I'll talk loudly when the popcorn begins to pop." This format allows the conversation to continue and develop in interesting ways.

- "Yes, but . . . " or even answering "yes" without the "and" is not enough. "Yes and . . . " plus another declarative sentence opens the scene to unlimited possibilities.

- Bring two volunteers to the stage in front of the audience.

- Ask the audience to propose a situation in which a group of people might find themselves and to identify the relationship of those people to each others. For example: workers and boss trapped in elevator, family picnic, strangers sitting next to each other at a ball game. After the situation and the identities of the players have been determined, ask Player 1 to begin with a declarative sentence, keeping in mind the relationship he has to the other players and the situation he is in.

- Continue the role play until it comes to a natural stopping point or until a predetermined time has been reached.

- Conclude the activity with the following questions:

  - What are the obstacles to agreement?

▲ How does it feel to be consistently agreed with?

▲ How can this technique be helpful to you in your dealings with others?

CREATIVE CONSULTANTS

 *A team has 5 minutes to come up with a name, target market, slogan, jingle, and spokesperson for a fictitious product.*

GOALS

To illustrate the power of total and unequivocal agreement and cooperation.

To demonstrate a technique for group problem solving.

To reveal how solutions to problems are built on previous ideas.

GROUP SIZE

Teams of 5–8 players.

TIME

10–15 minutes.

MATERIALS

Easel pad and markers; paper and pencils for each team.

> *This game works well with groups that have played* **Yes, and** . . . .

PROCESS

▨ Form teams of five to eight players. Have an easel pad available so ideas can be written down and seen by all of the participants.

▨ Allow room for players to move around as the creative process leads to pacing, shouting, and large physical gestures.

▨ Bring one team on stage and give the following instructions:

  ▲ As a creative consultant team you have contracted to design an advertising campaign for an exciting new product. You must create a name, slogan, and jingle for the product as well as choose a target market and an appropriate spokesperson. The ad components may be assembled in any order.

  ▲ The team must design the campaign in complete and total agreement. Negative thinking is not allowed. Each idea offered by a team member must be accepted and used.

  ▲ Players, the only way this can be accomplished is to accept each idea mentioned by any team member. If Player 1 shouts out an idea for a name, no further discussion of the name is allowed. Only one suggestion for each topic is necessary because the first one is always accepted and used. Move on to another topic.

  ▲ Team members, praise each idea loudly and enthusiastically by roaring "Yes! Great idea!" or something similar every time a suggestion is offered.

  ▲ At this time select one player to be the team secretary to write down and keep track of the ideas.

  ▲ Audience, choose a product the team will work on. Pick an ordinary item and add an unusual quality to it. For example, crackers whose crumbs are magnetized for easy cleanup, socks that whine when more than a foot away from their mates.

Multiple teams may work on the same product or a different one from other teams. Have easel pad or paper and pencils available for each team.

▲ You will have 5 minutes to create the entire ad campaign.

▨ Signal the team or teams to begin.

▨ Call time after 5 minutes and reconvene the entire group. Lead a closing discussion using the following questions:

▲ How is it possible to create a solution to a problem through agreement only?

▲ What are the difficulties in working this way? What are the benefits?

▲ Is the solution likely to be better or worse than one arrived at after extensive brainstorming, discussion, and analysis?

▲ What mind-sets and thinking patterns need to be overcome in order to be successful?

▲ How many of the obstacles to success are in our behavior? How many in the behavior of others? What can we do with this information?

VARIATIONS

▨ Add or substitute other items such as package design, media placement, premiums, ad or TV commercial copy, or a product demonstration.

▨ Choose a problem relevant to the participants.

LIST 5

Players stand in a circle. The player who is "it" must list five items in a designated category before an object travels around the circle.

GOAL
Practice relaxation, concentration, and focus while under pressure.

GROUP SIZE
5–20 players. Adjust the number of list items to the size of the group.

TIME
10–20 minutes.

PROCESS
▪ Have an object ready that can be quickly and easily passed around a circle of people. For example, a rolled up magazine or a whiteboard eraser.

▪ Prepare a list of categories that contain at least five items. Make the categories challenging (five state governors, five spices, five songs with a color in the title) while being neither too easy (five states, five foods, five colors) or too hard (five official state songs, five foods on the Titanic's menu). If you plan to use this game regularly, keep a variety of categories and lists handy. You may find the need for a list with as few as three items on it for a small group or as many as ten items for a large group.

- Arrange the players in a circle. With more than fifteen players, use more than one circle. Have an object for each circle to pass around.

- Stand in the center of the circle or between the circles if there is more than one.

- Hand the object to be passed to one of the players and instruct the players to start passing the object around the circle by giving it to the person on their right.

- Continue with the following instructions:

  - Keep the object going around the circle while I talk.

  - I will soon shout, "freeze." Whoever has the object at that moment is "it."

  - That player must immediately pass the object on and then list five items in a category I supply.

  - Player 1 must complete the list before the object goes completely around the circle.

  - If you succeed, come into the center and give the next category.

  - If you don't succeed, the player in the center remains, sends the object around again, and chooses a new category.

- Make certain the object is in motion around the circle, close your eyes, wait a few seconds, and yell "freeze."

- Continue the game until time is up. Conclude the activity with the following questions:

  - What were some of your thoughts, feelings, and actions while you were "it?"

  - This game allows players who are not "it" to observe how other players deal with pressure, frustration, and deadlines. Did you learn anything by watching others handling pressure and expectations?

VARIATIONS

- Adjust the number of answers in a category depending on the number of participants.

- **Hot topic:** Stand in the middle of the circle, choose a broad category, and toss an eraser or other safe object to one of the players. Category examples include song titles, four-legged animals, and states. The player must name as many items in that category as possible. When the player can no longer add to the lists, he throws the object to another player in the circle who must continue naming items in the same category, without repeating any. The game is over when a player takes too long to come up with an answer or repeats an item. Each player must list at least three items before throwing the object.

NUDGE, NUDGE

 *During this visually exciting, energizing exercise, players adopt a series of characteristics based on choices that other players make.*

GOALS

To loosen up the entire group.

To lose feelings of self-consciousness.

To experience being both the center of attention and giving up being the center of attention.

GROUP SIZE

Unlimited.

TIME

15–20 minutes.

MATERIALS

4 chairs in a row, in front of the group, facing the audience.

> *This game is simple, but the instructions sound complex. You may need to demonstrate the process.*

PROCESS

▨ Introduce the goals of the exercise to participants. Select four volunteers from the group to begin this activity and identify them as Players 1, 2, 3, and 4. Give the following instructions so all can hear:

▲ Player 1, stand facing the chairs. When I tell you to begin, adopt a physical or vocal mannerism, such as flailing arms or barking, or combine the two and walk toward the end chair on your right. Continue your chosen mannerism as you approach and sit in the chair. Keep up the mannerism while you are seated.

▲ After Player 1 has been in the chair for a few seconds, Player 2, approach the same end chair with a different mannerism or sound than Player 1.

▲ Player 1, as Player 2 approaches the chair, slide over one chair to the right, continuing your sounds and actions.

▲ Player 2, sit in the chair Player 1 vacated and continue your actions. After a few seconds, Player 2, gently nudge Player 1 while saying, "nudge, nudge."

At this point, both players are sitting in chairs making their own sounds and actions.

▲ Immediately upon being nudged, Player 1, adopt the actions or sounds of Player 2. Continue this way as Player 3 begins to approach.

▲ Player 3, approach the end chair as Players 1 and 2 shift over a seat.

▲ Player 3, sit down and continue with your own action for

a few seconds then nudge Player 2 who will adopt your actions.

- ▲ Player 2, after a few seconds nudge Player 1 who will also adopt Player 3's actions.

- ▲ Player 4, with a new and different action, repeats the pattern.

- ▲ We'll continue in this round-robin fashion until everyone who wants to participate has had a turn.

- ▲ During this activity, focus your attention on staying with your own action until it's time to shift smoothly to a new act when you are nudged.

- Reconvene the entire group and begin a closing discussion with the following questions:

- ▲ What makes this game so much fun?

- ▲ At any point, did you feel silly or foolish? If so, were you able to overcome this feeling? How?

- ▲ Did you experience any resistance entering into or leaving an activity?

PASS THE PULSE

Holding hands while seated in a circle, the group sends a pulse around the circle in a toppling domino style.

GOALS

To foster team spirit.
To practice focusing and centering.
To experience the flow of information.
To make a physical connection with other team members.

GROUP SIZE

8–50 participants.

TIME

5–15 minutes.

PROCESS

▓ Seat the group in a circle, preferably cross-legged on the floor, with knees almost touching those of the player on either side. Include yourself as part of the circle. Allow players with any physical discomfort to sit as they wish. It can also be done with the group standing in a circle. The important thing here is the hand-holding.

■ Give the following instructions:

▲ Hold hands with the people on both sides of you. Hold their hands loosely and comfortably. You will remain in this position for the next few minutes.

▲ Firmly and gently, squeeze the hand of the player to your right. This is the action you will need to play this game.

▲ The game will begin when I squeeze the hand of the player on my right. As soon as that player feels my squeeze in her left hand, she will squeeze the left hand of the player on her right with her right hand. That player will then squeeze the hand of the next player and so on around the circle until the pulse returns to me.

▲ The object of the game is to send the pulse through each player and complete the circle.

▲ The most effective way to play is to wait until you feel the squeeze in your hand before passing it on. Picture your left hand as a receptor of information. It can do nothing but receive the input. It cannot make the input arrive faster nor has it any control over what happens to the input before it arrives.

▲ The pulse must be passed on as a conscious decision rather than an automatic reaction. The mission is to successfully transmit energy and communication. It is not to see how fast we can go around.

▲ The right hand gives the information. Its intention is to tell your partner that the information has arrived and it is time to send it on around the circle.

- The player on your right is completely dependent on you for correct information. If your right hand twitches, an incorrect message may very well be sent around the circle.

- Let's first send the pulse around the circle slowly and deliberately so we can see how it works. I will begin and when it returns to me I'll send it around again at a quicker pace.

Squeeze the hand of the person on your right and watch to see that the players have the idea. The placement of the pulse within the circle should be fairly evident at any time since only one person should be squeezing at a time. Achieve one successful, full rotation of the pulse to make sure all understand the game.

Continue for a few orbits, then ask the players to close their eyes and keep passing the pulse. Continue the game until the pulse has successfully gone around a few times or until you'd like to move on.

Conclude the activity by squeezing both hands and holding the squeeze until all players are firmly squeezing each other's hands.

Relax your hands, then conclude with the following questions:

- You need only attend to your left hand. Why is that true?

- What is the benefit of staying in the moment in this game?

- In communication, absorbing input is crucial. What conditions help you absorb input in order to be effective in communication? What conditions hinder you?

- Were you patient or impatient waiting for the pulse to get to you?

- What was your self-talk as you waited?

VARIATIONS

Multiple pulses: After a pulse has left you and is on its way, send another pulse after it. This encourages players to stay more focused than with a single pulse. A modification to this variation is to send out a number of pulses and keep track of how many come back. To do this, send out all the pulses before the first one comes back to you. In a small group, you may have three to five pulses at a time. I've been in a group of fifty that had eleven pulses going at once. That leader only received six back. He used that information to emphasize how loss of focus affects group success.

Pass the clap: Instead of a pulse, a hand clap is passed. Players sit or stand with their left hand palm up and their right hand palm down. The leader begins by clapping her right hand with the left hand of the player to her right. That player then uses his right hand to clap the left hand of next player.

Pass the sound: Instead of a pulse, a sound is passed. Holding hands is not necessary. The leader begins by facing the player on her right. She makes a sound with an accompanying facial gesture. Player 2 faces the next player and intentionally passes the sound and gesture as identically as possible. The game continues until the sound has returned to original player.

COOPERATION MACHINE

One player goes on stage and demonstrates a repetitive movement. One at a time, other players come on stage and add their own repetitive movements in a complementary way. The result resembles a smooth-running machine.

GOALS

To reinforce the concept and power of teamwork.
To foster cooperation.
To pay attention to what other people are doing.

GROUP SIZE

5–25 participants.

TIME

10–25 minutes.

PROCESS

▨   Before beginning the game, make certain that the stage area is large enough to accommodate all the members of a group.

■ Pick a volunteer player from the group to be Player 1 and bring the player to the stage. Provide the following instructions:

▲ Player 1, begin a repetitive motion of some kind. You may pantomime donning and doffing a baseball cap; you may rub your belly in a satisfied way; or you may hop three feet to your left, then three feet to your right. Whatever you do, continue the pattern. Add sound to your motion, if you wish.

▲ After Player 1 has established a routine, becoming the first part of our cooperation machine, any group member can choose to be the next player to enter the game.

▲ Player 2, integrate yourself into the action by establishing an action that is complementary to Player 1's action. If Player 1 is facing the audience while rubbing her belly and making beeping sounds, you may choose to stand behind her, raise your arms when she beeps, and lower them when she pauses. Alternately, you may stand with your back to her, pat yourself on the head and say, "zoom" in between her beeps.

▲ Your objective is to integrate your sounds and movements with those of Player 1.

▲ When Players 1 and 2 have established a routine together, a third player, Player 3, will enter the stage and proceed to integrate a new action and/or sound into the presentation.

▲ Players continue, one by one, to contribute to the growing machine being represented by the other players. Each player must come in with the intent of integration and cooperation.

■ After all players have participated, conclude this portion of the game by asking the following questions:

- Why did the machine work so smoothly even though each player was working individually?

- Was everyone involved with the same activity? How do you know?

- How did you know what to do when you became part of the machine?

■ Select another volunteer and give the following instructions:

- Begin a repetitive motion of some kind, just as Player 1 did earlier.

- As before, any time after Player 1 has established a routine, any group member can choose to be the next player to enter the game.

- Player 2, this time enter the game with the intention to act in an incompatible or contradictory way to Player 1's action. You may choose to ignore Player 1 and start an action away from him; you may attempt to block his movements; or you may try to drown out his sounds.

- After Player 1 and Player 2 have been on stage for a few moments, other players may approach one by one. Players, come to the stage with the intention of working contrary to all the other players.

- Continue this way until all who want to participate have had a chance.

■ Lead a closing discussion using the following questions:

- What was the difference between the first game and the second one?

- When our intention is to be complementary to others, we

attempt to fit in. When our intention is to be incompatible, the result resembles chaos.

▲ Even if you don't know what your task is, going into it with the intention of seeing what others have done and acting in a complementary manner guarantees progress.

▲ What implications does this hold for us?

RESOURCES

RESOURCE LIST

Atkins, Greg. *Improv!: A Handbook for the Actor.* Heinemann, 1995.

Close, Del, Charna Halpern, and Kim Johnson. *Truth in Comedy: The Manual of Improvisation.* Meriwether Publishers, 1994.

Fluegelman, Andrew. *The New Games Book.* Dolphin Books, 1976.

Johnstone, Keith. *Impro: Improvisation and the Theatre.* Theatre Arts Books, 1989.

Jones, Brie. *Improve with Improv: A Guide to Improvisation and Character Development.* Meriwether Publishers, 1993.

Nachmanovitch Stephen. *Free Play: Improvisation in Life and Art.* J.P. Tarcher, 1991.

Newstrom, John and Edward Scannell. *Games Trainers Play.* McGraw-Hill, 1989.

Spolin, Viola. *Improvisation for the Theater: A Handbook of Teaching and Directing Techniques.* Northwestern University Press, 1983.

———. *Theater Game File.* Northwestern University Press, 1989.

Sweet, Jeffery. *Something Wonderful Right Away.* Limelight Editions, 1987.

Van Oech, Roger. *Creative Whack Pack.* United States Games Systems, 1993.

Weinstein, Matt. *Playfair: Everybody's Guide to Noncompetitive Play.* Impact Publishers, 1983.

Williamson, Bruce. *Playful Activities for Powerful Presentations.* Whole Person Associates, 1994.

ADDITIONAL TRAINERS RESOURCES

MIND-BODY MAGIC
Martha Belknap, MA

Make any presentation more powerful with one of these 40 feel-good activities. Handy tips with each activity show you how to use it in your presentation, plus ideas for enhancing or extending the activity, and suggestions for adapting it for your teaching goals and audience. Use *Mind-Body Magic* to present any topic with pizzazz!

- ❏ **Mind-Body Magic / $21.95**
- ❏ **Worksheet Masters/ $9.95**

INSTANT ICEBREAKERS
50 Powerful Catalysts for Group Interaction and High-Impact Learning
Sandy Stewart Christian, MSW, and
Nancy Loving Tubesing, EdD, Editors

Introduce the subject at hand and introduce participants to each other with these proven strategies that apply to all kinds of audiences and appeal to many learning styles.

Step-by-step instructions and dazzling graphics on the worksheets make any presentation a breeze.

- ❏ **Instant Icebreakers / $21.95**
- ❏ **Worksheet Masters / $9.95**

CREATING A CLIMATE FOR POWER LEARNING
37 Mind-Stretching Activities
Carolyn Chambers Clark, EdD, ARNP

Creative warmup processes that prepare leaders and participants for a satisfying learning experience. These activities will enhance your presentation skills, leadership style, and teaching effectiveness no matter what your audience or setting.

- ❏ **Creating a Climate for Power Learning / $21.95**

PLAYFUL ACTIVITIES FOR POWERFUL PRESENTATIONS
Bruce Williamson

Spice up presentations with healthy laughter. The 40 creative energizers in *Playful Activities for Powerful Presentations* will enhance learning, stimulate communication, promote teamwork, and reduce resistance to group interaction.

- ❏ **Playful Activities for Powerful Presentations / $21.95**

To order: call 1-800-247-6789

ADDITIONAL GROUP PROCESS RESOURCES

WORKING WITH WOMEN'S GROUPS, Volumes 1 & 2
Louise Yolton Eberhardt

When leading a women's group, don't just rely on personal experience and intuition—equip yourself with these volumes of proven exercises. Louise Yolton Eberhardt has distilled more than a quarter century of experience into nearly a hundred processes addressing the issues that are most important to women today.

The two volumes of *Working with Women's Groups* have been completely revised and updated. *Volume 1* explores consciousness raising, self-discovery, and assertiveness training. *Volume 2* looks at sexuality issues, women of color, and leadership skills training.

❏ **Working with Women's Groups, Vols 1 & 2 / $24.95 each**
❏ **Worksheet Masters, Vols 1 & 2 / $9.95 each**

WORKING WITH MEN'S GROUPS
Roger Karsk and Bill Thomas

Working with Men's Groups has been updated to reflect the reality of men's lives in the 1990s. Each exercise follows a structured pattern to help trainers develop either onetime workshops or ongoing groups that explore men's issues in four key areas: self-discovery, consciousness raising, intimacy, and parenting.

❏ **Working with Men's Groups / $24.95**
❏ **Worksheet Masters / $9.95**

WELLNESS ACTIVITIES FOR YOUTH, Volumes 1 & 2
Sandy Queen

Each volume of *Wellness Activities for Youth* provides 36 complete classroom activities that help leaders teach children and teenagers about wellness with a whole person approach and an emphasis on FUN. The concepts include: values, stress and coping, self-esteem, personal well-being, and social wellness.

Curriculum developer Sandy Queen designed these whole-person, "no-put-down" activities for kids from middle school to high school age, but many can be adapted for families or even for the corporate setting.

❏ **Wellness Activities for Youth, Vols 1 & 2 / $21.95 each**
❏ **Worksheet Masters, Vols 1 & 2 / $9.95 each**

To order: call 1-800-247-6789

TOPICAL GROUP RESOURCES

WORKING WITH GROUPS ON SPIRITUAL THEMES
Elaine Hopkins, Zo Woods, Russell Kelley, Katrina Bentley,
and James Murphy

True wellness must address the spirit. Many groups that
originally form around issues such as physical or mental
health, stress management, or relationships eventually
recognize the importance of spiritual issues. The material
contained in this manual helps health professionals initiate discussion
on spiritual needs in a logical, organized fashion that induces a high
level of comfort for group members and leaders.

❑ **Working with Groups on Spiritual Themes / $24.95**
❑ **Worksheet Masters / $9.95**

WORKING WITH GROUPS TO OVERCOME
PANIC, ANXIETY, & PHOBIAS
Shirley Babior, LCSW, MFCC, and Carol Goldman, LICSW

Written especially for therapists, this manual presents well-
researched, state-of-the-art treatment strategies for a
variety of anxiety disorders. It includes treatment goals,
basic anxiety-recovery exercises, and recovery enhancers
that encourage lifestyle changes. Sessions in this manual are related
directly to the chapters in *Overcoming Panic, Anxiety, & Phobias.*

❑ **Working with Groups to Overcome Panic, Anxiety, & Phobias / $24.95**
❑ **Worksheet Masters / $9.95**

WORKING WITH GROUPS TO EXPLORE
FOOD & BODY CONNECTIONS
Sandy Stewart Christian, MSW, Editor

This collection of 36 group processes gathered from experts
around the country tackles complex and painful issues nearly
everyone is concerned about—dieting, weight, healthy
eating, fitness, body image, and self-esteem—using a whole
person approach that advocates health and fitness for people of all sizes.

❑ **Working with Groups to Explore Food & Body Connections / $24.95**
❑ **Worksheet Masters / $9.95**

CREATIVE PLANNING FOR THE SECOND HALF OF LIFE
Burton Kreitlow, PhD, and Doris Kreitlow, MS

This is the first book to help group leaders design a
presentation or workshop that addresses the whole-person
needs of people ages 50 and up. These 29 structured
exercises explore ways of planning for retirement by finding
intriguing ways to make a useful life for yourself—not
simply setting aside money for the day you quit working.

❑ **Creative Planning for the Second Half of Life / $24.95**
❑ **Worksheet Masters / $9.95**

To order: call 1-800-247-6789

WORKING WITH GROUPS FROM DYSFUNCTIONAL FAMILIES
Cheryl Hetherington

This collection of 29 proven group activities is designed to heal the pain that results from living in a dysfunctional family. With these exercises leaders can promote healing, build self-esteem, encourage sharing, and help participants acknowledge their feelings.

❑ **Working with Groups from Dysfunctional Families / $24.95**
❑ **Worksheet Masters / $9.95**

WORKING WITH GROUPS ON FAMILY ISSUES
Sandy Stewart Christian, MSW, LICSW

These 24 structured exercises combine the knowledge of marriage and family experts with practical techniques to help you move individuals, couples, and families toward positive change. Topics include divorce, single parenting, stepfamilies, gay and lesbian relationships, working partners, and more.

❑ **Working with Groups on Family Issues / $24.95**
❑ **Worksheet Masters / $9.95**

WORKING WITH GROUPS IN THE WORKPLACE

BRIDGING THE GENDER GAP
Louise Yolton Eberhardt

Bridging the Gender Gap contains a wealth of exercises for trainers to use in gender role awareness groups, diversity training, couples workshops, college classes, and youth seminars.

❑ **Bridging the Gender Gap / $24.95**
❑ **Worksheet Masters / $9.95**

CONFRONTING SEXUAL HARASSMENT
Louise Yolton Eberhardt

Confronting Sexual Harassment presents exercises that trainers can safely use with groups to constructively explore the issues of sexual harassment, look at the underlying causes, understand the law, motivate men to become allies, and empower women to speak up.

❑ **Confronting Sexual Harassment / $24.95**
❑ **Worksheet Masters / $9.95**

CELEBRATING DIVERSITY
Cheryl Hetherington

Celebrating Diversity helps people confront and question the beliefs, prejudices, and fears that can separate them from others. Carefully written exercises help trainers present these sensitive issues in the workplace as well as in educational settings.

❑ **Celebrating Diversity / $24.95**
❑ **Worksheet Masters / $9.95**

To order: call 1-800-247-6789

STRESS AND WELLNESS RESOURCES

STRUCTURED EXERCISES IN STRESS MANAGEMENT, VOLS 1–5
STRUCTURED EXERCISES IN WELLNESS PROMOTION, VOLS 1–5
Nancy Loving Tubesing, EdD, Donald A. Tubesing, PhD,
and Sandy Stewart Christian, MSW, Editors

Each book in these two series contains 36 ready-to-use experiential learning activities, focusing on whole person health (body, mind, spirit, emotions, relationships, and lifestyle) or effective stress management.

Developed by an interdisciplinary team of leaders in the wellness movement nationwide and top stress management professionals, these exercises actively encourage participants to examine their current attitudes and patterns. All process designs are clearly explained and have been thoroughly field-tested with diverse audiences so that trainers can use them with confidence.

Each volume brims with practical ideas that mix and match, allowing trainers to develop new programs for varied settings, audiences, and time frames. Each volume contains **Icebreakers, Action Planners, Closing Processes,** and **Group Energizers**. The *Wellness Promotion* volumes also include **Wellness Explorations** and **Self-Care Strategies.** The *Stress Management* volumes include **Stress Assessments, Management Strategies, and Skill Builders.**

> ❑ **Stress or Wellness 8 1/2" x 11" Loose-leaf Edition—Vols 1–5 / $54.95 each****
> ❑ **Stress or Wellness 6" x 9" Softcover Edition—Vols 1–5 / $29.95 each**
> ❑ **Worksheet Masters—Vols 1–5 / $9.95 each**
>   ** Worksheet Masters are included as part of the loose-leaf edition.**

STRESS AND WELLNESS REFERENCE GUIDE
A Comprehensive Index to the Chalktalks, Processes, and Activities in the Whole Person Structured Exercises Series
Nancy Loving Tubesing, EdD, Editor

This handy index is your key to over 360 teaching designs in the ten-volume *Structured Exercises in Stress and Wellness* series—organized by theme, time frame, level of self-disclosure, trainer experience level, and goals. This book includes all ten Tips for Trainers sections, with workshop outlines and suggestions especially for the workplace.

The *Stress and Wellness Reference Guide* makes it easy to plan a workshop by mixing and matching exercises suitable to your audience. You'll find easy-to-read charts with a quick view of group processes and activities—so you can find your favorites to use with any group.

> ❑ **Stress and Wellness Reference Guide / $29.95**

To order: call 1-800-247-6789